ANXIETY IN RELATIONSHIPS

YOUR PARTNER THINKS YOU'RE GREAT

How To Overcome Your Insecurities To Form A Stable Emotional Attachment To Your Partner With Strong Relationship Communication Skills Without Couple Therapy

NICHOLAS HOLTZ

from the Publisher. All additional right reserved.

The information in the following pages is broadly considered to be a truthful and accurate account of facts and as such any inattention, use or misuse of the information in question by the reader will render any resulting actions solely under their purview. There are no scenarios in which the publisher or the original author of this work can be in any fashion deemed liable for any hardship or damages that may befall them after undertaking information described herein.

Additionally, the information in the following pages is intended only for informational purposes and should thus be thought of as universal. As befitting its nature, it is presented without assurance regarding its prolonged validity or interim quality. Trademarks that are mentioned are done without written consent and can in no way be considered an endorsement from the trademark holder.

Table of Contents

PART I

Chapter 1: Anxiety, The Monster Within

"I know what it's like to be afraid of your own mind."

-   Dr. Reid from Criminal Minds

- Obsessing over small worries that constantly distract you
- Whirling from action to action to try to quiet your minds' nagging
- Attempting to drown out anxious thoughts in any way possible, solemnly wishing they would just disappear

If you are here with us today, you are likely living through all the above and more, trying strategy after strategy to eliminate these causes of stress. Or, perhaps you are seeking help for a loved one that has anxiety that is weighing them down. Or, maybe you are simply here to feed your curiosity of what anxiety is and how it plagues the mind. No matter, I work with anxiety every day and have spent the majority of my existence on Earth immersed in it.

My grandfather was such a worrier that he physically shook, *constantly*. His body would tremble from the overwhelming magnitude of worry that lurked within him. He was a burly southern man who favored anything outdoors and fishing. His long, curly locks framed his rounded face with an always generous smile. When he was at his warmest, he was a magnet to others. However, his most natural state was when he was in worry mode.

What did he worry about? Anything and everything. He was worried about all the typical things that grandparents do; along with I'm sure many countless unspoken things.

"Do you have enough to eat?"

"Do you need the salt or pepper?"

"Are you comfortable? Too hot? Too cold?"

Even though he was a burly man, his voice was soft, so anyone listening had to lean in. I think he like the intimacy it afforded. Whenever we were all at ease, he was at ease.

Us grandkids always ran with the joke, *"Grampy, can we pass you the salt and pepper?"* His anxiousness would disappear with a smile and flush of embarrassment. We did this to show our appreciation, to relieve the tension and let him know he was never a burden and that we loved our big burly gramps for who he was.

Our gramps was a people-person, always curious and invested in others. I have very clear memories of coming home and hearing his low but small voice in the answering machine, *"Hello, it is just me again. Just checking in to see how you are coming along…"*

He needed that regular assurance that everything was, in fact, alright and always preferred to hear it firsthand. And if he could do things for someone, that was even better.

As Gramps aged, his anxiety escalated and he became less able to use it in a constructive manner. There were less and fewer ways for him to release his anxious feelings, to the point he became crippled with worried on a daily basis. When I search into where my own anxiety stemmed from, a picture of Grampy always pops into my mind. When I studied anxiety in graduate school, his shaking body was a perfect analogy. The more time I spent exposed to the study of anxiety in the human body, I began to understand my grandfather better than he likely understood himself most days. I also realized how persuasive anxiety was throughout our family's history. It was what set the foundation for me to deeply understand how much anxiety affected emotions and behaviors.

Thankfully, no one else in my family shook as much as my grandfather did from anxiety; however, looking back, anxiety was the hub of all the spectrum of extremes my family endured. My mother was motivated by her anxiety, while my father was like a balloon, letting stress and anxious feelings build up until he popped with rage.

While no one in my immediate family was ever diagnosed with an anxiety disorder, I can still imagine that just like so many others, they would have felt the same shameful stigma that comes along with all mental health problems, thinking that something is wrong with them. They were simply noticing things in their lives and felt deeply about them; they just didn't have the tools and knowledge to cope with the overload of information.

Through my years as a psychologist, I have gained a different perspective on anxiety and how it alters thoughts and feelings. I have come to see anxiety as a resource and seek to embrace its value in our everyday lives.

Anxiety derives from the feeling of realizing that something we genuinely care about may be at risk, as well as the arrival of resources that we need in order to protect it. Anxiety prompts us to look closer and pay better attention to messages we receive and helps us to gain the motivation we need to take control of situations. The key to getting back a life driven by anxiety and fear is to take control. This is where I have used my knowledge to help others, in ultimately steering them in a different direction of gaining back their willpower.

How Anxiety Overshadows Everyday Lives

Living in denial, second-guessing your every move, thinking ill thoughts about your future, living in fear of the unknown; all these things can overshadow a person's life and lead to constant anxiety.

If you or a loved one is plagued by anxiety, you have probably endured panic attacks and constant negative nagging in your head on a regular basis or have a phobia of some kind feel ashamed of their "sickness."

Anxiety has the power to make everyday folks feel insane, even though they truly aren't. Just like with all people, some days are better than others, but those who experience symptoms caused by these mental ailments typically have a higher count of bad than good days.

They often feel that they are always under a dark cloud that pours rain, but that rain is not made up of just water. Those drops from the sky above their head are created from startling visions, disturbing logic, feelings of worthlessness and/or hopelessness and looks that they receive from both loved ones and strangers when they truly believe they are in a type of personal crisis or feel as if they are about to be pushed over the edge. This is just a small portion of what it is like to live with anxiety.

What is Anxiety?

Anxiety, in its simplest form, is a bodily reaction to unfamiliar or dangerous environments and scenarios. Everyone has the tendency to get anxious from time to time and feel distressed or uneasy. This happens perhaps before a big game, performing in front of an audience or right before a huge job interview. Feeling anxious is a natural response that our bodies can feel during moments like these. Anxiety gives us the boost we need to be consciously aware and alert to prepare us for certain situations.

Our body's "fight-or-flight" response is under this umbrella of reactions. But imagine feeling like this *all* the time, even during the calmest of moments?

Picture a life where you have issues concentrating on everyday tasks, where you may be frightened to leave the safety of your home when you cannot fall or stay asleep because your mind is in a constant whirlwind of thought? Living with an anxiety disorder is debilitating. That is putting it lightly in some cases.

Causes of Anxiety

Every one of us is unique, which means even common disorders, like anxiety and depression, resonate within each of us differently, as well as why we are living with anxiety, to begin with. There are several key factors that cause anxiety disorders to grow in the mind:

- Chemistry of the brain
- Environmental factors
- Genetics
- How we grew up
- Life events

The factors listed above are the basics that lay the groundwork to potentially be a victim of anxiety, but those below mixed with any of those above could set one up to be someone that is at a higher risk than others in the development of an anxiety disorder:

- Alcohol, prescription medication or drug abuse
- Chemical imbalances in the body and/or brain
- History of anxiety that runs in family bloodlines
- Occurrence of other mental health issues
- Physical, emotional or mental trauma
- Side effects one has on particular medications
- Stress that lasts an extended amount of time

The feelings and thoughts that anxiety promotes within a sufferer create a bubble that creates lonely thoughts and feelings, which is why it is no surprise that anxiety disorders are the most common of mental illnesses with the U.S, with **_over 40 million American adults_** living with one of these disorders as we speak.

If it is any consolation, you are by no means alone when it comes to feeling the way you do. There is still a lot of research being put into finding out why anxiety plagues so many individuals, its specific causes and why it resonates within individuals in such vast ways.

Signs & Symptoms of Anxiety Disorders

All of us will experience anxiety in our lives; it is a normal response to stressful life events. But as you have learned so far or experienced for yourself, these symptoms can become much larger than the events of stress them and can interfere heavily with a happy, healthy way of life.

Below are the most common symptoms of anxiety:

- **Worrying** that is disproportionate to the events that trigger it and is intrusive, making it challenging to concentrate on everyday tasks.

- **Agitation** that causes fast heartrates, sweaty hands, dry mouth, etc.

- **Restlessness** or feeling on edge with a constant uncomfortable urge to move that won't go away.

- Becoming **easily fatigued**, either in general or after a panic attack.

- **Difficulty focusing** on everyday tasks.

- **Issues retaining short-term memory** which results in a lack of performance in multiple areas of life.

- Becoming **easily irritable** in the day to day life.

- Constantly having **tense muscles** that may even heighten anxious feelings.

- **Issues falling and staying asleep** due to continued disturbances in the sleep cycle.

- **Panic attacks** that produce overwhelming sensations of fear.

- **Avoidance of social situations** due to a fear of being judged, humiliated, or embarrassed.

- **Extreme fears** about very specific situations or objects that are severe enough to interfere with normal functioning.

Understanding Social Anxiety

Imagine at random times, feeling so uncomfortable in particular situations to the point of not being able to process what is happening around you or difficulty breathing. Welcome to the life of those that deal with social anxiety. Social anxiety is classified by a major discomfort with social interactions as well as a fear of judgment. There are more than 15 million Americans that deal with this in their everyday lives that struggle with the awkwardness of social settings.

Symptoms of Social Anxiety

The main symptoms of this form of anxiety are feeling intensely anxious when in social situations or avoiding them altogether. Many sufferers have a constant feeling that 'something just isn't right', but are never able to pinpoint it.

As you can imagine, these people have a twisted way of thinking that includes false beliefs of situations and negative opinions from others. Many people fear the interaction days or weeks before the event, which means that social anxiety can manifest in other physical symptoms, such as:

- Sweating
- Shaking
- Diarrhea
- Upset stomach
- Muscle tension
- Blushing
- Confusion
- Pounding of heart
- Panic attacks

The key aspect of social anxiety to remember is that even though these folks have a fear of speaking or interacting with others, it doesn't mean they have nothing to say.

Below are things that those who suffer from social anxiety would say to others to help them understand how they feel:

"I do not want this and I cannot help it. It is not just a bit of nervousness that comes and goes. It is constant stress and living in a world that you start to not recognize."

"In my ability to speak right, I lack confidence. There are many times I want to say something, but hold back because I am afraid of how dumb it may sound or that I will be misunderstood. I am afraid of speaking in groups, phone calls, and approaching people the most.

"I am terrified of people's reactions when I do scrounge up the courage to finally speak."

"My anxiety socially is not a constant. There are certain situations that cause me more anxiety than others. It is a fluid disease."

"Many times, people don't realize that those with this anxiety disorder are suffering because of the lack of physical symptoms. Just because you cannot tell there is something wrong, doesn't mean there isn't."

"I cannot help how ridiculous it may seem."

"It hurts to know that people take my anxiety personally instead of just helping me out."

"I wish I had a social life, but my anxiety won't let me; I am not anti-social."

"It may look like I am zoning out from time to time, but I am actually practicing positive self-talk and breathing techniques to stay calm and ward off a panic attack."

"I am not trying to be standoffish, rude, or snobby, even though it may seem that way when I refuse hugs or don't wish to speak. I simply get overwhelmed and overstimulated easily. All I ask for is respect."

"I want people to break the ice and speak to me first. I am genuinely a nice person, I just have a fear I am unable to control."

"I wish more people understood that when I say I cannot come, it is because the situation I was invited to feels 'impossible', not because I don't feel like it."

"When I leave early, I am not being disrespectful. I just need to fight off a meltdown with some alone time."

"Social anxiety is not 'shyness'; that is like comparing a stab wound to a paper cut."

No one experiences social anxiety in the same way. Each day is like living a life of constant fear; worrying about the disapproval of others, rejection, not fitting in, etc. They are bound to be anxious to enter or begin a conversation.

Chapter 2: Acknowledging Your Anxiety

While the numbers of those that suffer from anxiety in the United States alone exceed 40 million, you may feel alone in your symptoms as well as what triggers them. Things that set off those anxious thoughts and feelings are a bit different for everyone who experiences anxiety. It is important to take time to focus on yourself and learn what things provide you with peace or create tension in your life.

Common Anxiety Triggers

- The hustle and bustle of everyday life. Life is always busy and there never seems to be time to slow down.
- The inevitable fact that we are only growing older.
- Driving, especially on freeways with many cars or across bridges.
- Not living up to the expectations that we set for ourselves.
- The sense of uncertainty. When we are not on control of situations we tend to freak out a bit. This comes from a lack of communication and anxiety making conclusions for us.
- Ambulance, fire or police sirens.
- Stresses at work – Not performing well enough, not having enough time during the course of the workday to get things done, etc.
- Simply thinking about what triggers your anxiety can be a cause for anxiousness in itself.
- Being too hot is often times directly associated with being claustrophobic.
- The inevitable part of life known as death. This especially goes for individuals who have experienced much loss in their lives.
- Being alone.

- The possibility of finding out that people do not like you as much as you think they do.
- Being judged or verbally attacked.
- Large crowds.
- The inability to predict the future. Those with anxiety often dislike surprises.
- Trying new things.
- Being far away from home or other places familiar to you.
- When many people speak to or at you all at once.
- The struggles that your children may face at school.
- Money! This is a big one. Whether it is saving for a big event such as a wedding or purchasing a home or car, the process of paying monthly bills while still trying to save money for other things.

Getting to the Root Causes of Your Anxiety

What many of us do not realize is that many causes that trigger our anxieties to flare up are actually self-produced. While you can blame your situation, family, friends, etc. for you distress, you are the one who perceives life as it goes on around you. The way you view it, analyze and take it all is all dependent on you. The root reasons behind the curtains of 'Play Anxiety' are usually caused by one of the following reasons.

Negative Self-Talk

It is said by research conducted by behavioral specialists that upwards of 77% of all the things we think to ourselves is quite counterproductive and negative. What we don't realize is that we are being our own worst critic and a detriment to ourselves. Learn to become consciously aware of the way you speak to yourself.

Write down any sort of negative thoughts for a day and then each day forward practice transforming those negative words or thoughts into a happy, loving one towards yourself. While it may feel weird at first, it will become second nature to you once you practice it for a while. Your self-talk is just as important of a daily habit as any other.

Unrealistic Expectations

Sometimes we simply just have too high of expectations that create a high world that we struggle to reach. Expecting those to be perfect and remember all the details about you is just ridiculous. If your expectations fly way above you, you are more than likely missing out on grand opportunities and are unable to truly recognize the good things that are happening that you should be celebrating.

This goes for the expectations you have for yourself as well. Are they actually realistic? If not, how can you go about making them more reasonable and achievable?

The "Should" Thoughts

Do you find your brain thinking that you "should do this" and you "should do that" often? Have you ever just taken a moment to actually find the reasoning behind why you "should"? Telling yourself that you should is equivalent to telling yourself that you are not good enough. It leads to negative self-talk fast and should be avoided. Make a positive list of the things you should do or become. Are they yours or someone else's expectations?

Taking Things Too Personally

Those with anxiety feel like many things that occur are actually their fault when in reality they more than likely had nothing to do with someone's disgruntled behavior or a glare they received. Learn to not take things too personally because you never know what may be happening in the life of other people.

"We are all in the same game, just different levels. Dealing with the same hell, just at different devils." If you think you are the cause of someone's actions, speak up and ask instead of just assuming. This will get rid of a lot of assumptions that go into negatively feeding your anxiety.

Our minds are wired to believe the things that we tell it the most. If we are always engaging in negative self-talk, expect too much of others or ourselves, do things we just merely think we "should" do or worry about those around you, your brain will act negatively as well. It is all about building a positive foundation for your frame of mind for all those thoughts of yours to dwell in. In order to unlock the door to happiness and less stress and/or anxiety, it is time to get thinking in a happy manner!

Pinpointing Your Anxiety

While you can take all the time in the world to read information in regards to relieving anxiety via the internet, books or other media, unless you take action and decide that you truly want to make a change to lower your anxiousness, it will never happen. I am an anxiety sufferer and back just a couple years ago it engulfed my everyday life and drowned me more than a few times.

I finally over time came up with a process that assisted me greatly with determining what triggered my anxious thoughts so that I could get a grip on my life and yield them from continuously taking over my personal life.

- **Stop** – When those feeling of anxiousness begin to hit you, stop and take a moment to make a mental note of what you are doing right at that moment. This is easier said than done, for you might be in the middle of a task, conversation, etc. But it is beneficial to take just a moment to identify when you began to feel anxious.

- **Identify** – Recognizing the onset of anxiety will help you come to the conclusion of what actually causes it for you personally. If you develop the capability to notice triggers and feelings when they start to dwell, you can put a stop to them faster. Many people don't realize they are feeling anxious until their symptoms are outrageously taking over them. Over time, you will be able to catch on more quickly what is threatening your happiness and overall well-being.

- **Write** – As you become an expert of taking moments to make mental notes of why you feel anxious, I find that at the end of the day I write down the events during my day, both the goods one and those that triggered my anxiety. I keep a notepad on my cellular device so that I am quickly able to access it to jot down notes at the moment and then write them down on paper before heading to bed. Be sure to write down as many details as possible – what you are thinking, experiencing and feeling, etc.

- **Analyze** – At the end of the week is when I choose to review what I have written in my anxiety notebook. You can review it at the end of each day, week or month, but I do not recommend waiting any longer than that. I wait at least a couple days to a week so that I can see the pattern that my thoughts made. When you are aware of these patterns you are better able to focus on the causes of anxiety and avoid them.

- **Possibilities** – There are numerous things that you can make the scapegoat when it comes to feeling anxious. If you have adequate knowledge of these ideas, you can review patterns and conquer anxiety. Anxiety in many cases is situational. If you are anxious being in unfamiliar surroundings, expose yourself to these types of circumstances a little time. If your causes are more based on the way you think and view the world, learn to engage in positive self-talk. Once you have a pattern written out, you will be less anxious just by the fact that you have some idea and control over your anxiety situation overall.

Chapter 3: Trauma and Anxiety

The journey of life is exciting, scary, ridiculous, confusing and worth it all at once. But there are times that we all go through some type of emotional distress, whether it be mere sadness, rapid anxiety, addictions to outside influences, obsessions with things or people, compulsions we have a hard time controlling, behaviors that are self-sabotaging, physical injuries, anger, and bleak moods, among the hundreds of other things we go through, think and/or feel.

It is important to learn ways to cope when it comes to hard times, no matter the time frame. Something psychologically downgrading can happen in a matter of mere moments and leave you scarred for the rest of your life. Some people seek out help from other individuals who are professionals at understanding the human mind, but others wish to find help within them. Having the knowledge to help yourself is not an easy feat. It may be easy to read pages upon pages of books and self-help websites that provide information, but it is much harder to put those words into actions.

The world is a much different place now than it was just a decade or two ago. Technology has advanced so rapidly that some of us are overwhelmed with it all, especially the consequences that we receive, whether from our own actions or that of another being who acted upon a current mood. Human beings are not the robots that we seem to want to create so badly these days. We are emotionally driven individuals with a lack of having the knack to help ourselves in times of need and/or trouble.

The worst thing about the constant rise of this distress is the fact that there is no one age group or certain targeted individuals that are more likely to go through it. It is happening clear from late grade school levels all the ways into senior living years. Students have much more stress with perpetual levels of testing and pressure to be better. Employees live their hard-earned careers always fighting to make their way up the ladder with not much reward. Older individuals are continuously having their wages and retirement that they worked their entire lives for whisked away.

It is a dog eat dog world out there with a lot of room to make mistakes that can cause even more friction in our personal lives. With the constant pressure to be better than the next, our society has taught us maybe how to be more proficient in terms of getting things done at school or work, but many of us have forgotten the person that is truly important: OURSELVES. If we do not take care of our emotional health, detrimental things can occur. Below are some signs that you may be experiencing emotional distress. Some of the symptoms may surprise you.

Childhood Trauma and Sensitivity to Anxiety

Trauma during childhood can impact our entire lives. According to the Journal of Affective Disorders, children who experience traumatic situations are much more likely to have anxiety and depressions and fall victim to alcohol and drug abuse. The same study found that females are more susceptible than males to develop anxiety, even with the same rates of trauma.

If left untreated, trauma during childhood can have effects that last throughout someone's entire life. They are likely to developmental disorders that branch out to much more than just anxiety as well.

Common Anxiety Disorders Caused by Trauma

Common anxiety disorders that are caused by traumatic events are:
- Panic disorder
- Obsessive Compulsive Disorder (OCD)
- Post-Traumatic Stress Disorder (PTSD)
- Body Dysmorphic Disorder

- Agoraphobia
- Social Phobia(s)

As you can imagine, trauma anytime throughout your life can play a major part in the development of anxiety and other mental disorders in your lifetime.

Chapter 4: Grabbing your life back from anxiety

Now that you have acknowledged that life could be better and have learned how to interpret why you live a life filled with anxiety, it is time to take your life back, pronto! There is a variety of methods we will discuss in this chapter that can help you gain back the confidence you need to live life to the fullest.

Managing Your Emotions

Emotions are a natural human phenomenon. , and are very present in pressing and painful times. Every day we are driven by some force of emotions:

- We take chances because we get excited about new opportunities
- We cry because we are hurting and make sacrifices for those we love

Those are just a couple examples of emotions; they dictate our actions, intentions, and thoughts with authority to our rational minds. Emotions can become a real problem, however, when we act too fast or we act on wrong types of emotions, which cause us to make rash decisions.

Negative emotions, such as bitterness, envy, or rage, are the ones that tend to spiral out of control the most, especially when triggered. It only takes one slip of our emotions to totally screw up the relationships in our lives.

If you have issues controlling your emotions, here are some steps that you can implement into your everyday life that will help you regain rationality, no matter what challenging situation you are facing:

Don't react right away

You are more likely to make mistakes when you react right away to emotional triggers. When reacting right away to these triggers, you are likely to say and do things that you will later regret.

Before acting on emotions, take a deep breath to stabilize your impulses.

Breathe deeply for just a couple minutes and you will be able to feel your heart rate return to normal. One you become calmer, remind yourself that feeling this way is just temporary.

Find healthy outlets

Once you have managed your emotions, you need to learn how to release that build up in the healthiest way possible; emotions are something that you should never let bottle up. Talk to someone you trust. Hearing their opinion of the matter can help to broaden your thoughts and regain control.

Many people keep a journal to write down how they feel. Others engage in exercise to discharge their emotions. Others meditate in order to return to their tranquil state. Whatever activity suits you, find it and use it when emotions get high.

Look at the bigger picture

All happenings in our, both bad and good, serves a purpose in our lives. Being able to see past the moment strengthens your wisdom. You may not understand certain circumstances right away, but over time, you will see the bigger picture as the pieces of the puzzle fall into order. Even when in an emotionally upsetting time, trust that there is a reason that you will comprehend in time.

Replace your thoughts

Negatively fueled emotions create negative recurring thoughts that create cycles of negative patterns over time. When confronted with these emotions, force them out of your mind and replace them with more positive thoughts. Visualize the ideal ending playing out or think about someone or something that makes you happy.

Forgive your triggers

Triggers could be the ones you love the most; you're best friend(s), your family, yourself, etc. There will be times that you may feel a sudden wave of rage when people do things that annoy you or a self-loathing feeling when you remember back to the past when you could have done thing differently. The key to managing your emotions is to first, forgive. This allows you to detach from your jealousy, fury, and resentment. As you forgive, you will discover that disassociating yourself from these feelings will do you the best.

Every day we are constantly reminded of how strong and prominent our emotions are and the power they have. We are bound to take the wrong action from time to time and feel the wrong things. To avoid acting out, simply take a few steps back and calm your spirit that is heightened from outside forces. You will be grateful for mastering your emotions when it comes to building and strengthening meaningful relationships.

Using the Power of Mini Habits

Just after Christmas in the days ending 2016, I was reflecting on the year. I realized that I had tons of room to improve but always failed at keeping up with my New Year's resolutions. Instead, I decided that in 2017, I would explore other options.

On the 28th of December, I made the choice that I wanted to get back in shape. Previously, I hardly if ever exercised and had a consistent guilt about it. My goal was a 30-minute workout, realistic, right?

I found myself unmotivated, tired, and the guilt made me feel worthless. It wasn't until a few days later that I came across a small blog article about thinking the opposite of the ideas you are stuck on. The clear opposite of my 30-minute workout goal was chilling on the couch, stuffing my face with junk food, but my brain went to the idea of 'size.'

What if, instead of carrying that guilty feeling around all the time, I just performed one push-up? I know, right? How absurd of me to think that a single push-up would do anything to help me towards my goal.

What I found was a magical secret to unlocking my potential...when I found myself struggling with my bigger goals; I gave in and did a push-up. Since I was already down on the floor, I did a few more. Once I performed a few, my muscles felt warmed up and I decided to attempt a pull-up. As you can imagine, I did several more. And soon, I exercised for entire 30-minutes!

What Are Mini Habits?

Mini habits are just like they sound; you choose a habit you want to change and you shrink them down to stupidly small tasks.

For instance, if you want to start writing at least 1,000 words per day:

- Write 50 words per day

- Read two pages of a book per day

Easy, right? I could accomplish this in 10 to 20 minutes or so. You will find that once you start meeting this daily requirement, you will far exceed them faster than you would imagine.

What is *More* Essential than Your *Habits*?

You might be wondering how you can become more comfortable in your skin and be yourself in a cruel world with these so-called mini habits. Well, think about it; what is more important than the things you do each and every day? NOTHING. Habits are responsible for 45% of how we behave, making up the foundation of who we are and how happy we are in life.

The main reason people fail to change anything in their life, even the aspects they know need to change is because they never instill new habits. Why? Simply because in the past, they have tried to do way too much, all at once. If establishing a new habit requires you to have more willpower than you can muster, you are bound to be unsuccessful. If a habit requires less willpower, you are much more likely to succeed!

Benefits of Mini Habits

There are many additional benefits that come with utilizing mini habits in your everyday life. Here are a few:

- Consistent success breeds more success
- No more guilt
- Stronger productivity
- Formation of more positively impactful habits
- Generation of motivation

Chapter 5: Belittle anxiety with personal empowerment

Having a negative attitude towards life keeps us from being happy and impacts those that we interact daily with. Science has more than enough proof to show how being positive impacts your levels of happiness and terms of success. This is why making positivity a habit with the help of small changes can help you to drastically change your overall life and the mindset you have towards the world. The life you are living is a direct reflection of your overall attitude. It can be quite easy, almost too easy, to be cynical at the world and see it as a mess of injustice and tragedy, especially thanks to the media that we all spend many hours a day on.

Negativity is holding you back from really enjoying your life and has a great impact on your environment as well. The energy that people bring to the table, including you, is very contagious. One of the best things you can do in your life that is free of charge and simplistic is to offer your positive attitude. This is especially beneficial in a world that loves and craves negativity.

One of my favorite quotes of all time comes directly from the King of Pop, Michael Jackson: *"If you want to make the world a better place, take a look at yourself and make a change."*

As humans, we are creatures of habit. In this chapter, we will outline small but significant changes that can be made to form positive habits that can drastically change the overall mindset of your life around.

Smile

When asked who we think about most of the time, the most honest answer would probably have to be ourselves, right? This is natural, so don't feel guilty! It is good to hold ourselves accountable and take responsibility for ourselves.

But I want to challenge you to put yourself aside for at least one moment per day (I recommend striving for more) and make another person smile.

Think about making someone else happy and that warm feeling you get when you receive happiness. We don't realize how intense the impact of making someone smile can have on those around us. Plus, smiling costs nothing and positively works your facial muscles!

Focus on solutions, not problems

Embracing positivity doesn't mean you need to avoid issues, but rather it is learning how to reconstruct the way you criticize. Those that are positive create criticisms with the idea to improve something. If you are just going to point out the issues with people and in situations, then you should learn to place that effort instead into suggesting possible solutions. You will find that pointing out solutions makes everyone feel more positive than pointing out flaws.

Notice the rise, not just the downfall

Many of us are negative just by the simple fact that we dwell too much on the hate and violence that is in our daily media. But what we fail to notice is those that are rising up, showing compassion, and giving love to others. Those are the stories you should engulf yourself in. When you able to find modern-day heroes in everyday life, you naturally feel more hopeful, even in tough times.

Just breathe

Our emotions are connected to the way we breathe. Think about a time that you held your breath when you were in deep concentration or when you are upset or anxious. Our breath is dependent on how we feel, which means it also has the power to change our emotions too!

Fend off other's negativity

I'm sure you have gone to work cheerful and excited to take on the day ahead, but then your co-worker ruins that happy-go-lucky mood of yours with their complaints about every little thing, from the weather to other employees, to their weekend, etc.

It is natural to find yourself agreeing to what others are saying, especially if you like to avoid conflict. But you are initially allowing yourself to drown in their pool of negative emotions. Don't fall into this trap.

Conflict may arise, but I challenge you to not validate the complaints of a friend, family member, or co-worker next time they are going about on a complaint-spree. They are less likely to be negative in the future if they have fewer people to complain to.

Switch the "*I have to*" mindset with "*I get to*"

I am sure you often fail to notice how many times we tell ourselves that we have to go and do something.

- "I have to go to work."
- "I have to go to the store."
- "I have to pay rent."
- "I have to mow the lawn."

You get the picture. But watch what happens when you swap the word have with the word get.

- "I get to go to work."
- "I get to go to the store."
- "I get to pay rent."
- "I get to mow the lawn."

See the change in attitude there? It goes from needing to fulfill those obligations to be grateful that you have those things to do in your life. This means:

- You have a job to go to
- You have enough money to support yourself and your family to provide a healthy meal
- You have a roof over your head
- You have a nice yard

When you make this simple change, you will begin to feel the warmth of happiness snuggle you like the cold blanket of stress falls away.

Describe your life positively

The choice of vocabulary we use has much more power over our lives than we realize. How you discuss your life is essential to harnessing positivity since your mind hears what you spew out loud.

When you describe your life as boring, busy, chaotic, and/or mundane, this is exactly how you will continue to perceive it and it will directly affect both your mental and physical health.

Instead, if you describe your life as involved, lively, familiar, simple, etc., you will begin to see changes in your overall perspective and you will find more joy in the way you choose to mold your entire life.

Master rejection

You will need to learn to become good at being rejected. The fact of the matter is, rejection is a skill. Instead of viewing failed interviews and broken hearts as failures, see them as opportunities for practice to ensure you are ready for what is to come next. Even if you try to avoid it, rejection is inevitable. Don't allow it to harden you from the inside out.

Rethink challenges

Stop picturing your life being scattered with dead-end signs and view all your failings as opportunities to re-direct. There are little to no things in life that we have 100-percent control over. When you let uncontrollable experiences take over your life, you will literally turn into mush.

What you can control is the amount of effort you put into things without an ounce of regret doing them! When you are able to have fun taking on challenges, you are embracing adventure and the unknown, which allows you much more room to grow, learn and win in the future.

Write in a gratitude journal

There are bound to be days where just one situation can derail the entire day, whether it be an interaction that is not so pleasant or something that happens the night before the day ahead, our mind clings to these negative aspects of the day.

I am sure you have read on multiple sites about how keeping a gratitude journal is beneficial. If you are anything like me, I thought this was total rubbish that is until I started doing it. I challenged myself to write down at least five things that I was truly grateful for each and every day. Scientifically, expressing gratitude is linked to happiness and reducing stress.

I challenge you to begin jotting down things you appreciate and are grateful for each day. Even on terrible days, there is something to be blessed about!

Chapter 6: Everyday techniques to fend off anxiety

Despite the toll that anxiety and its symptoms can have on everyday life and fulfillment, in today's world there are many different techniques and methods you can learn to incorporate into your everyday routine that help you to control and possibly even eliminate anxiety from your life. Each section of this chapter will be dedicated to a specific genre of techniques that anyone has the ability to learn!

Visualization and Anxiety

Seeing *is* believing, which is a key secret to how entrepreneurs and well-known people in society stand out and achieve success and fulfill their dreams. *Visualization is the simple use of imagination through mental imagery to help form visions of what we want in our lives and how we can make them a reality.*

There are two main kinds of visualization:

Pragmatic Visualization represents a set of days that helps to gain new ideas and interpret what it says/means to them. It helps those understand structures that lie within a set of data.

Artistic Visualization is similar to pragmatic in that it utilizes visuals to convey information but in a different sense. It is used to show people that data is being monitored carefully and shows particular aspects of data that is connected to one another to depict an entire idea.

So, how does learning about these two kinds of visualization help you in your quest to decrease anxiety? Well, visual techniques help to drastically overcome symptoms of anxiety. When the two types are combined, visualization is powerful in obtaining and staying in a calmer state of mind.

When it comes to anxiety, visualization requires one to picture themselves in a safe, peaceful and/or tranquil environment. Anywhere that makes you happier is where you should be imagining yourself during visualization exercises. It does sound pretty funny at first glance, but trust me when I say there is something about being able to transport your mind to somewhere mentally tranquil. Not only will your mind thank you but your body will too, for it becomes much more relaxed and stress-free when performing these practices. Visualization gives people something to distract themselves from the current world that surrounds them.

Why You Should Be Using Visualization

Beyond visualization itself, you can literally view the best of life from the comfort of your own couch. This chapter will showcase the benefits that come with the dedicated practice of learning and incorporating ways of visualization into your everyday life.

- **Improved quality of relationships** – The positive outcomes of utilizing visualization doesn't just end within yourself. Since you are developing a better mindset that aids in your views and beliefs, those around you will like and appreciate the more confident, positive you!

- **Boosts your mood** – When one practices the methods of visualization, they naturally experience a sort of joy that is quite unexplainable to some. Once you finish one of these sessions successfully, you will more than likely feel boastfully happy, calm and relaxed.

- **Relieves stress** – Practicing the ways of visualization naturally causes one to be able to relax. It has a way of quieting the mind to be able to think happier, more positive thoughts which tone down loads of stress that pile on our shoulders almost on a daily basis.

- **Strengthens the immune system** – Thanks to all that dialing down of stress and things that fuel stress, your body is better able to fight off sickness which makes you physically better, longer. This also helps in aiding anxiety because you are not constantly worrying about getting ill all the time as well.

- **Ability to learn new things quicker** – When the mind is in a calmer state, it is able to pick up and grasp new concepts much easier than when it is bogged down with so many negative thoughts and emotions.

- **Able to cope with the feeling of nervousness** – When you take time out of your day to practice visualization, you are initially settling all those negative feelings that you may have about yourself and what others may think of you as well. This immensely helps individuals who are naturally more nervous combat that feeling, which leaves room to try and experiment with new things and ideas. Imagine yourself in a great looking outfit giving that inevitable speech that is due soon. Then imagine an applauding audience. It is quite the confidence booster!

- **Builds stronger concentration skills** – Visualization makes room for your mind to do other tasks efficiently by spring cleaning negative thoughts, feelings, emotions, and past experiences. This doesn't mean it is responsible for getting rid of them 100%, but it helps one to be able to cope and bring down those bad levels to make room for productivity.

- **Assists in overcoming recurring issues** – When the weight of your entire world is upon your shoulders, it is no wonder that we begin to believe that our lives were just made to be a laughing-stalk to some because of how life's unlucky events have left us feeling. This can lead to long-term problems and beliefs. Visualization combats these two things.

- **Can give you a spark of inspiration** – During your sessions, if your mind always veers to one idea in particular, perhaps it is time to take initiative and proceed with the steps in achieving it! Visualizing doing something can directly inspire you to do as such.

- **Makes one more creative** – Visualization not only takes concentration but also a truckload of creativity as well. If you are going to picture something in detail and add the other four senses to that visual, you have to really want to mold it into reality. We all have creative bones in our bodies. Visualization just brings them out more, honing that skill and letting it shine.

- **No boundaries** – As I have mentioned before, when it comes to visualization, practice makes perfect. Just like with any newly acquired skill, one must learn to hone its practice to be able to tweak it when needed and use it to their utmost advantage. With certain visualization techniques, you can literally picture yourself doing something that would otherwise be usually hard to achieve. With those images in mind, you then have a good idea what you must do to actually and realistically accomplish that image you had in your head during a visualization session. This method knows no bounds!

- **Method of practice and rehearsal** – Believe it or not, visualization can be a way to practice your favorite sport or nail that upcoming work pitch that you have been reciting and memorizing for days. Picturing yourself doing or performing something is just as effective as actually completing the task at hand. Utilizing visualization with real, physical practice can get you to honing that skill or memorizing things much quicker.

- **Picture yourself getting stronger and healthier** – Sounds unbelievable, but if you are sick, seeing yourself get better will have the result of getting healthier, sooner. Visualization reduces stress and relaxes your mind, which also assists in healing your body of sickness or physical injury as well. This allows your body to function at its full capacity. You would be surprised what our bodies could accomplish in a day's work if we treated them more like the temples they are and should always be. It is safe to say we take our physical presence for granted most days. And it tends to show more often than not!

- **Gives us joy** – Many people who practice the ways of visualization tend to picture something that brings them happiness. We almost are never quite in the right place or time in our lives to always have what we want and that is okay! But that doesn't mean we shouldn't get the luxury of seeing it for ourselves, right? Picturing a goal or what we want the most from life can bring us quite a load of temporary happiness if one wants to view it that way. Why temporary? If you can picture it, you can eventually and more than likely make it happen in your future, which is why visualization can be a great motivator.

Aspects of Successful Visualization Practices

There are three aspects to successfully become one with visualization:
- **Practice** – Learning the ways of visualization may actually be more stressful and frustrating for beginners because it is not a practice we are naturally keen to perform. Those that start practicing visualization have a false sense of what the experience is supposed to feel like and have false expectations about the outcome. This inhibits the practice from really taking effect. Visualization is something that has to be practiced daily to work for you long-term. If practiced the right way, it will eventually become second nature to you but only if you really dedicate yourself to learning its ways and practicing it every day until

you have it down pat.

- **Utilizes ALL the senses** – Visualization doesn't just use your sense of how a certain peaceful place appears to you in your mind. You have to imagine what your safe space smells, tastes sounds and feels like as well. The more detailed you are in regards to your senses, the better visualization you will have and the more relaxed you can potentially become.

- **Actions** – All human beings experience mental barriers that keep them from being happy and the process of practicing and performing visualization is not excluded from this. Even for visualizing experts, bad thoughts from the course of one's day can inhibit one from getting a clear vision of their safe haven. You have to find a way to release and/or transform those bad thoughts and feelings into something that you can tangibly get rid of.

Forms of Visualization for Anxiety

Visualization is a skill that can be utilized to obtain a better life, especially for those that suffer from an anxiety disorder. Now, we will talk about techniques in the visualization world. Although all of these are not for everyone, try them out and see what works for you.

Meditation

Meditation is a superb form of apathetic visualization that can lead to very powerful results. Visualizing through means of meditation is more of an outgrowth than the main focus. When you begin to incorporate meditation sessions into your everyday routine, you will gradually be opening the door to your inner self, which will then lead you to be able to visualize more clearly and easily.

The more experience you have with meditation, the smoother sessions become and the more you get to see and take away from your visions. It is important not to become frustrated with yourself or discouraged from continuing to practice meditation if you are just starting out.

The whole point of meditation is to empty your brain of thoughts and feelings and to let your mind wander to wherever it wants to go. A vital component of meditation is breathing. Learn to focus on how you take in and let out breaths of air. Let your mind veer off to wherever its little heart desires. Once you begin to practice this technique more often, it will become easier and faster to exhaust your mind of concerns or other worries and let other things come in and explore. It will become second nature for you to sit down, relax and get into a clear state of mind so that you can visualize to your contentment.

Meditation makes way for things that you never thought were actually within you. Once you rid your brainwaves of all that noise from the course of your day, thoughts occur at their own pace.

Altered Memory Visualization

This visualization technique targets past memories and learning how to change them to a more positive standpoint. For those with anxiety about things that stem from their past, this is especially helpful in obtaining a brighter state of mind. This technique is one to utilize if you are one that holds on to past anger and resentment from particular situations that you finally want to rid yourself of.

No one can change the past, but you can teach your brain how it views these past scenarios in your mind. Get into a calmed state and visualize the scenario that you wish had a different outcome. Restore things said that were fueled by anger with comments that are controlled and peaceful. This does take some time and you may have to revisit this scene in your head multiple times to nail the outcome that you wish had resulted from the past situation. It is recommended to not do this day upon day in a row, but rather space out revisiting the scene.

Over time, your brain will begin to only recall what YOU have recreated, making a once painful or uncomfortable situation fade away in memory. Try to imagine little cubicle offices in each major section of your brain. In this instance, I like to picture a little office guy that is in charge of just the bad memories. During these sessions, you are instructing him on how to rewrite particular events that have occurred in the past and once they are rewritten the way you once anticipated them to play out, this office dude can start to shred your memories of these occurrences.

Receptive Visualization

This technique is much like viewing a movie inside your head, but you are the director of the scenes within this movie. Get yourself to a quiet space, lie back, get comfortable and close your eyes. Focus on building the scene in which you want to see acted out in your mind.

Once a clear backdrop and scenery is within your mind, place people, noises, smells and sounds within your scene of this movie. It is best to slowly build your way up to the actual scene until you are comfortable and content with it, then it is time for action! Focus on feeling involved within this scene of your "movie."

Treasure Map

This visualization technique not only uses mental fundamentals but also physical components as well. You will need to have an idea of what you want to visualize before getting to the nitty-gritty of performing this method. Start by using your art skills to draw out some type of physical representation of the components you need to achieve in order to reach your ultimate goal.

For example, perhaps you have an upcoming test that you want to get a great grade on. Draw out a building symbolizes a school, a book that you will need to use to study for this test and then a representation of yourself. Try to make your drawing detailed, but do not worry about the maturity of your art abilities too much here. It is not the drawings themselves that are important, but rather what you are imagining WHILE sketching them out.

As you draw out your "map to success", your mind is actually visualizing ways that will get you to where you want to be. Patience is a key with this particular technique, for it does take a bit of time to truly become completely mentally occupied in this exercise. It is crucial to take your notepad and pen to a quiet space and to not be around anything distracting such as a radio, television, people or phones.

How to Design Your Own "Safe Space"

Safe places or spaces are a mind's sanctuary, created for the purpose of retreat if one needs a mental location to be able to visualize or hone their meditative state and reduce stress. Creating one of these is kind of like personalizing a physical space in your home. You want to do anything to truly make it YOURS.

It can be anything from a room inside an imaginary home, a room in your realistic home that you want to visualize differently, the beach, a comforting outdoorsy area, etc. As you meditate or relax and begin to dive deeper into your imagery or visualization session, this is the place you imagine you want to go. It is anywhere that you wish to return to time after time, so put some effort and thought into where you will always find comfort in mentally retreating to.

- **Brainstorm** – The goal is to develop a place that you feel calm, content and happy within, no matter the reason that you retreat to it. If you have difficulty seeking out such a place, start by looking through art, magazines, books, old photographs, etc. Always lean towards ideas that burst with positivity for you.

- Are you more apt to feel calmer in an outdoor/natural setting or do you feel better within the walls of some type of structure?

- Are there pieces of writing such as within books, poems of stories that make you feel at ease?

- Do you feel more comforted by populated areas or tranquil areas?

- **Think of a time where you felt happy and safe** – Memories are the best areas to seek things that bring joy to you. Think back to memories that you were happy, content, playful, peaceful, etc. Write these down in detail. It could be literally anywhere, as long as it brought contentment to you.

  - Where did this memory occur?
  - How old were you?
  - Why did this memory make you happy?
  - Who was with you within this memory?

- **Create various rooms** – Your safe space does not necessarily have to be just 2D, one room vision. It can have various sections, compartments or rooms within it. This allows you to trek to different areas throughout your visualization sessions. This also allows one the ability to be able to compartmentalize issues and deal with them one part at a time.

  - *Fill your space with cherished people* – There are many individuals that would rather be alone while in their safe place, while others prefer the company of their favorite people. Imagine who makes you happy and during the course of a visualization session, imagine greeting them and welcoming them into your safe space. This also goes for people in your life that may have passed away that you miss and wish to see. Having conversations with them and asking for advice could make a world of difference!

- *Utilize ALL your senses* – Seeing is believing, but visions of your safe place are a lot more believable and turn in better results if you learn to engage all your senses while within them. Engulf yourself in tastes, sounds smells and how things feel between your fingers and toes and against your skin. It will enhance your visualization experience ten-fold.

- *Write out all the details* – Once you have taken the dedicated time to develop and build your safe place, write down all the tiniest details that you can remember. Writing in a lot of detail can assist you in returning to that place in your mind easier and more efficiently. Some individuals even videotape, sculpt, draw or paint out their descriptions for safekeeping for future use.

  - Are there animals or people?
  - What do you feel?
  - How small or big is your space?
  - What colors?
  - What surrounds you?
  - What is the ultimate backdrop or setting?

- **Visualize positive results** – The main rule of thumb for

51

visualization is imagining situations acted out in positive manners. This involves a heavy amount of thinking happily and setting up a content scene. Imaging positive outcomes are really just a more in-depth version of regular run-of-the-mill positive thinking.

Developing Anxiety Routines

Anxiety routines are any type of daily routine that you use to calm yourself down in stressful situations and that leaves you feeling physical, mental or emotionally distressed. These routines are meant to help you bounce back from the depths of your own thoughts and live a life full of more passion and fulfillment.

This means it is very crucial to choose routines that not only suit you but are healthy, too. Life runs smoother when you have a routine to fulfill those nasty little voices in your head or when you feel like you may make a bad choice because of your anxiety symptoms. Sadly, some people choose unhealthy habitual routines that not only push them back into a negative state but may even provoke symptoms of anxiety and make them worse.

These bad routines could be anything from drug use, both illegal and prescription, large consumption of alcohol or heavy smoking of cigarettes, etc. You get the picture. Creating an anxiety routine for yourself should not include things that will cause you greater harm in the long run. Honestly, habits like those stated above are only going to make your symptoms worse.

As human beings, we are automatically wired to detect any sort of negative energy that may cause us harm. Anxiety becomes so bad within certain people simply because our bodies do not quite know the difference between stressful triggers that are actually harmless to us versus actual, life-threatening aspects that may be sprung upon us.

Our bodies are made to react to protect ourselves. This is why being mentally prepared for the day that lies ahead of you is so crucial, especially for anxiety sufferers. It is important to back up our thoughts with an extra layer of positivity to promote a sense of safety and well-being. This is much easier said than done, especially when life may not have been a very good friend to you as of late. But being able to mentally develop a positive sense of self is the first step in creating daily routines that help pave your way to a successful life to live and your future.

Routines to Decrease Anxiety

With the right amount of inspiration, the first day or two of adding a new routine to your life can be exciting. You know you are making a positive change that will hopefully help you feel better about yourself and the life you live. However, self-care routines can be a hard thing to manage and utilize on a regular basis once the newness of acting upon it wears off.

Anxiety can leave some sufferers so dismayed by anxious or sad thoughts that they want nothing more than to do away with anything that resonates positive energy. But this is the exact opposite of fighting for yourself and your happiness. Everyone has their bad days and moments and by all means, you are allowed to have and live those. But it is important not to stay tucked away in them for long periods of time.

Developing and executing specific daily routines that you are comfortable with gives those a step by step plan for the day and keeps you prepared for situations or other anxiety triggers from leaping out and mugging you of your happiness. Routines, kind of like exercise, are things we practice daily to keep us in shape, but anxious routines keep our minds in check. You never know when something will catch you off guard, when a person may ask you something that is bothersome or when a debilitating symptom of anxiety will hit you throughout the course of the day. It is better to be prepared than not to be, right?

The Importance of a Balanced Morning Routine

Many functions within routines do them absolutely no good. When the alarm goes off, they tend to hit snooze a few times. When they finally decide to open their eyes, they automatically reach for their phones and look at updates on social media. Many people are already let down by the fact no one messaged them or liked their posts throughout the night.

When their feet finally touch the floor to stand up out of bed, they are already on a path to a negative, self-destructing day. They take a quick shower, down a bowl of cereal and chug a cup of coffee and get to their day job...what is the point?

This lack of routine is non-beneficial. We see our unstructured lives as having no real purpose, which results in a lack of inner peace. We are destroying our happiness without realizing it!

Benefits of a Morning Routine

Creating a morning routine is not only a big part in relieving anxiety, but it also boosts productivity, brings out your inner positivity, helps you to develop and successfully sustain good relationships, as well as being a big reducer of negativities. Morning routines alone have been shown to be the best strategy for reducing stress and relieving those pesky symptoms of anxiety, no matter how long they have resided within you.

Morning routines keep you consciously aware and more grounded throughout the day. In fact, many who were once stubborn and did not want to incorporate a daily routine were eventually surprised at how much better they felt each and every morning. Anxiety levels dropped and confidence and happiness levels substantially rose. A morning routine can literally reduce your anxiety by as much as sixty percent!

Steps to Include in Your Morning Routine

When you **wake up earlier,** you know that you have plenty of time to get up and get ready for your day, which aids in decreased stress levels. If there is adrenaline pumping throughout your body as you rush around to head out the door, it sticks with you for the rest of the day.

Sounds like a waste of time, but **making your bed each morning** is a powerful task that helps you gain the momentum you need to get pumped for the day ahead. For those that suffer from anxiety and depression, making the bed is simple but can make a huge difference because you know you have completed *one* task if not anything else.

Meditation and prayer is a subject with many critics. People view meditation as an act performed only by spiritual individuals. Practicing mindfulness daily has positive side effects that can trigger feel-good hormones in the brains that aid in reducing levels of stress, anxiety and even depression.

Mixing meditation and prayer within your morning routine can be quite vitalizing, giving clarity to your life and your decisions. If you wish to learn more about the power behind the act of prayer, it will be covered in the following chapter The Empowerment of Prayer.

Taking an ice cold shower in the mornings has been proven to provide the human body with a great number of benefits. Cold exposure, also known as cold shower therapy, is nothing new. Our ancestors utilized it as a remedy to treat mental ailments. Showering in cold water provides the body with adequate circulation and tones the skin nicely.

The cold feeling kicks positive responses throughout the body into overdrive. It accelerates the repairing of cells, which reduces inflammation, pain, and speeds up our metabolic processes. The icy waters help lower negative levels that depression and anxiety can hover over us. Standing under the cold water for just a couple minutes can yield you these benefits.

Substitute your breakfast with coffee or tea to bump up energy levels and replace your usual breakfast eats. This is not recommended for absolutely everyone, but if you are trying to find ways to keep hunger away for the first portion of your day, give it a shot!

Learn how to **utilize a journal** to make "morning pages" as part of your routine in the mornings. This is my personal favorite way to "mind dump" any curious or troubling thoughts you had during the previous day and the night before, as well as random ideas that pop into your mind. I write in my journal after taking a shower, since great ideas tend to spring during those few minutes. When you are able to write down all the negative feelings on paper, you can then get through the day with a clearer state of mind.

Practice gratitude by jotting down things you would miss if they were no longer in your life, such as objects, people, etc. into your morning pages.

To start the day on a positive note, **jot down what you are looking forward** to that day. This tells our brains to look up, think up and be bright and helps to relieve anxiety.

Write down your intentions at the beginning of each day, no matter how corny they may sound, such as *"I will choose to be consciously present today."*

Write out important tasks that you wish to achieve during the day to ensure you will feel prepared and have a fulfilling plan. This will ease your mind so that you can develop a clear path of action to achieving that days' goals.

I know I have mentioned writing a lot, but like I said before it is a powerful tool. Every morning our brains are ready to go and on high alert, so it is good to have a well-thought-out plan of action.

Write down at least three to five of the most important tasks that you have to complete. Focus on ones that stress you out just thinking about them. Then, ask yourself the following questions about the tasks you have jotted out so that you can prioritize them accordingly:

- Which tasks will help me inch closer to achieving my main goal?

- What task do I have the most fearful anxious thoughts about?

- Which tasks have the potential to cancel out others if done successfully?

Spend 90 minutes every day working towards accomplishing your priorities. Targeting your main goals during the morning hours help you to get them accomplished productively.

Other Morning Methods to Relieve Anxiety

Play uplifting music to ensure an upbeat, positive mood. Create a playlist to play throughout your morning routine. Make your phone's alarm tone a good song to wake up to. You would be surprised at what a difference this effortless step takes.

Spend time with a pet(s) to help raise your dopamine and serotonin levels, resulting in lessened anxiety and depression. Pets also motivate us to climb out of bed and give us the initiative to take on the day, even when our anxiety tries to get the best of us. Adding them to your morning routine is a bonus for not only you but for your pet's well-being too!

Change your scenery in simple ways; Go outside, take a walk. Visit your favorite café and grab a coffee. Go out with a friend. The longer you dwell in a space that sucks away happiness, the worse you will feel.

Interactions with the outside world can be enough to distract you from your anxious habits. This is another reason routines are so important in aiding anxiety. Avoiding responsibilities can actually damage you mentally more than you realize. It is good to get your attention off the darkness of life that resides inside your head. It only makes your anxiety worse when you sit around and obsess over it.

Coping with anxiety and its symptoms can lead to a life of great discomfort. Having some type of structure in the form of routines can be quite crucial to one's success in living a happy, go-lucky life. The next few chapters will cover other types of routines in detail that can help relieve and maybe even make your symptoms disappear for good! It is all about you to initiate making the change.

Chapter 7: Transforming Your anxiety for a better life

If you are feeling anxious or depressed about your future and are allowing negative thoughts to get the best of you and dampen your motivation for success, then learning to use anxiety to your advantage is a must.

Personally, I have learned to *choose* to view my anxiety has a valuable asset that yields me to lead a more authentic life. I live empathetically, for my anxiety has made me a vulnerable person and thus, helped me deepen my life's relationships.

Having anxiety just means I am not mellow enough to take things for granted in life, therefore, making life a richer experience all the way around. In fact, there are a few inspirational ways that anxiety has helped me to elevate my life:

- Got me actively involved in personal development
- Taught me how to think in the present and act now
- Got me reading more books and discover how it heals the mind
- Started me on tracking my success and not just on failure
- Taught me how to make a positive game out of my life
- Assisted me to take control over my life
- Reconnected me to the habit of learning new things every day
- Showed me the power of meditation and visualization
- Allowed me to see that I am not the only one in my life that suffers from degrees of anxiety
- Has taught me to be a more actively vulnerable person

Using Anxiety to Your Advantage

Believe it or not, anxiety can be used for good and can be a powerful force in motivating yourself to achieve your desires. Using stress to add momentum to your life is constructive, instead of allowing it to deconstruct our lives.

Redefining danger

You must learn to see anxiety differently; anxiety, before our brains get a hold of it and dwell, is just a warning sign used for our survival. At this point, you are allowing anxiety to make you feel panicked. But even when that warning sign lights up, it doesn't mean you are in danger. You must save this energy for when you really need to make quick decisions.

Create a list of less to most dangerous to help identify a good spectrum of threats. With that comparison, you will be able to see what "dangerous" situations are safe and which ones are frightening.

Channel your stress properly

Diamonds don't grow from trees; they are coals that turn into something more beautiful through pressure. Channeling stress positively into energy for motivation does take time and can be physically and emotionally draining. But instead of allowing negative thoughts take hold of you and send you down that same spiraling hole of anxiety, look at the situation before you differently; view it as your time to *shine*! When negativity starts to manifest in your mind, challenge those thoughts. When you challenge them, you will find that the negativity in them is totally empty in the first place.

Stop trying to do your best

There are two kinds of people: those that do their best and those that can *do better*. However, those that strive to do their best constantly are the ones that end up emotionally drained than those who do better. Why? Because when you do your best, you are settling. When you strive to *do better*, you accept that you are not doing as good as you know you can. For anxiety sufferers, what they do isn't good enough for them. They either drown in their shortcomings or have learned to take the opportunity to improve themselves.

In those with anxiety, underestimation is a common cognitive distortion. When we tell ourselves that we can do better, we know how to reject our deficiencies and go out of their way to prove themselves wrong.

Chapter 8: Battling anxiety like a true warrior

"The only thing we have to fear is fear itself."

- *President Theodore Roosevelt*

Marines, SEALs, and Special Forces have no choice but to face life-threatening danger head-on regularly. The fact is, if they do get caught up in fear, they are more likely to lose their lives. While many of us will thankfully never have to face these experiences, why aren't we using the fear-crushing tactics that they use in our own personal lives?

Spend time preparing

If you are worried about a work presentation, stressing over a job interview, or freaking out about the upcoming rap battle that might help you move out of your mom's house, then stop, prepare, and practice instead of sitting around. The key is to lose yourself in the moment, which you to by devoting a ton of energy into preparing for what you are worried about. Spend 75% preparing and 25% for the actual event.

SEALs are able to erase fear by practicing upcoming mission until they feel naturally confident. When the unknown becomes more known to them, they don't have to lie to themselves about the risks, but instead put themselves in a better position to handle the unknown, which develops confidence.

Learn to *manage* fear

One of the best ways to deal with fear is to laugh about it. What? You read that right! Laughter lets you know that things are going to be okay and work out. Don't worry; there is evidence to back this theory up. A study by Stanford University showed that those that were trained to make jokes to respond to negative images. This is a much healthier way to deal with fear. The world is an inevitably twisted place, so seeing the funnier side of things makes it easier to deal with.

Breathe

When your heart is beating from your chest, your joints turn into Jell-O, and sweat is pouring off your face, then the best thing you can do to calm the physical manifestations of fear derived from anxiety is to breathe.

That simple? YES. By just inhaling for four seconds and exhaling for four seconds, SEALs can calm their nervous systems and maintain control of their natural biological responses to fear.

You are essentially bending your body's software to better control the hardware. In other words, you are giving yourself a pretty bomb superpower! Breathing helps the body go from the fight-or-flight response of the sympathetic nervous system to the relaxed response of the parasympathetic nervous system.

Tactical breathing used by Navy SEALS for performance just prior to a tense situation or during a workout:

Breathe through the nose. It's very important to breathe through your nose since breathing through the nose stimulates nerve cells that exist behind sternum near the spine that triggers the parasympathetic nervous system. Anxiety is a sympathetic response and parasympathetic counteracts that. This calms your body, which then calms your mind.

1. Relaxed sitting position and right handle on the belly.
2. Activate the breath by pushing belly out and then inhale deeply for a count of four. Inhale to the belly. This pulls breath deep into the lungs. Exhale through the nose for a count of four, pulling the belly button toward the spine. Repeat this three times.
3. Now breathe in through belly and diaphragm for a count of four, again inhaling into your belly and this time lifting your chest. Again, exhale

for a count of four so that your rib cage falls and your belly button pulls toward your spine. Repeat three times.

4. Next, use the same technique, this time inhaling for a count of four through the belly, diaphragm and your chest, with a slight raise of shoulders for inhaling. Exhale for a count of four three the chest, diaphragm, and then the belly. Repeat three times, eventually working your breaths up to eight counts.

Next, box breathing is a technique used by the U.S. Navy SEALS to maintain focus and to calm nervous system after a tense situation, such as combat, an intense workout or anytime the desire is to center and focus.

Trains for diaphragmic breathing or deep breathing. Relaxes the whole system and provides oxygen to the brain to focus better. Improves energy. It can also be used by you to regain your sense of balance, concentration, and relaxation and can be practiced at any time. Use the same technique as tactical breathing but you use a five-count hold between breaths.

1. Get in a relaxed sitting position
2. Inhale deeply through the nose for five seconds
3. Hold the air in your lungs for five seconds
4. Exhale for five seconds, releasing all the air from your lungs
5. Hold your lungs empty for five seconds
6. Repeat for five minutes, or as long as you feel necessary

Don't keep things bottled up

Fear is just like terrible liquor; it sucks when you drink it and has negative effects that last a long time, which is why it is important to deal with it before and after the fact.

Talking about scary experiences helps soldiers locate the meaning behind it all. This communication allows them to process what they have been through positively and helps them to create closer relationships with their mates. Scared? Admit it to a friend. Hearing it out loud can help you pull it out, confront it, and deal with it.

Overpower that inner nagging voice

We are all aware of the inner chatter that occurs in our mind on a daily basis. In fact, our inner voice can be really negative the majority of the time. Wouldn't it be cool to have an inner monologue that reminds us how confident and awesome we are? Wouldn't it be great to have an inner motivational speaker to get us through tough times?

Well, you can. In times of stress, our brains are wired to create self-talk that can increase our feelings of fear. As a soldier, they are expected to fight against their inner self-talk and focus on positive portions of experiences. With practice, they are easily able to ignore or even erase the negativity their brains are throwing at them. So, you can do the same in your own life.

Fear and anxiety thrive when we imagine the worst. We developed imagination to be able to project into the future so we can plan ahead. However, a side effect of being able to imagine possible positive futures is being able to imagine things going wrong. A bit of this is useful; after all, there really might be muggers or loan sharks. But uncontrolled imagination is a testing ground for anxiety and fear that can spoil otherwise happy lives.

Some people misuse their imagination chronically and so suffer much more anxiety than those who either future-project their imaginations constructively or who don't tend to think about the future much at all. Anxious, chronic worriers tend to misuse their imaginations to the extent that upcoming events feel like catastrophes waiting to happen. No wonder whole lives can be blighted by fear and anxiety.

Think of the worst-case scenario

No matter what you are afraid of, you always have the opportunity to avoid it for the rest of your life. However, soldiers don't get that choice. They face similar situations time and time again that scare them. To ensure fear doesn't overrule them, they simulate stressful scenarios and try to experience the emotions with them as well.

Instead of thinking happy thoughts and ignoring what you are afraid of, start looking at the worst things that can possibly happen. When you are able to picture the worst fear and stay within an emotional experience instead of pushing yourself out of it, your mind tends to get over the fear naturally.

Reframe your mindset

Reframe you definition of symptoms. Reframe the symptoms of anxiety - give them a different meaning. Those sweaty palms, racing heart, and lightheadedness can mean a panic attack or they can mean the most exciting and fun adventure of your life! Your body doesn't know the difference and it is just doing what it does by nature, but you can choose how you define that sudden rush. Don't believe me?

How do you think those adrenaline junkies dives off cliffs, jump motorcycles or swim with sharks? Their definition of what we call fear is definitely different. They still experience the same potent chemicals coursing through their body, but the sensations have a different meaning to them. What you experience as fear, dread and near death can be defined as thrilling, exciting, and aliveness to someone else.

The beautiful thing about consistently and purposely redefining these symptoms is you can actually rewire your brain. . This leads us to neuroplasticity.

Neuroplasticity

Neuroplasticity occurs with changes in behavior, thinking, and emotions. With conscious practice, we can alter our neural pathways to move naturally towards our desired emotions, such as being thankful, calm, and happy and away from anger, stress, and panic.

As you choose to respond with positive emotion, you can strengthen the neural pathways to the desired emotions. As you make more neural connections over time to your desired emotion, the pathways to the negative reactions eventually become weaker and scrambled. This even works while using mental rehearsals of the situation and practicing your desired response.

Remember, this can also work in reverse. If you have a habitual response to circumstances, such as being angry in a traffic jam and you repeat these responses over and over in a high state of emotion, you will strengthen the neural pathways towards the emotion of anger in that situation. The masters over the centuries who taught positive thinking and faith may have actually been on to something and now we can prove it scientifically.

Get moving

Exercise is usually associated with weight loss, improved physical health, and a stronger immune system. But the benefits of exercise can expand much more. Exercise is just as important for your mental fitness as it is your physical health. Aerobic activity promotes the release of endorphins that are released in the brain and act as painkillers, which also help to increase a sense of well-being. Endorphins also improve energy levels, provide a better night's sleep, elevate your mood and provide anti-anxiety effects. Exercise also takes your mind off of your worries and breaks the cycle of negative thoughts that contribute to anxiety.

It is recommended to perform 30 minutes or more of exercise five days a week to have a significant impact on anxiety symptoms. You don't need a formal exercise program at the gym to experience these benefits. Light physical activity has been shown to have the same effects, including gardening, housework, washing the car and walking around the block. These can be done in small intervals throughout the day.

It's more important to do some sort of physical activity on a consistent basis than to aim for something that is not sustainable. Be realistic and if you need to start with smaller goals, do so. This is all about taking care of yourself in a way that works for you.

The single, most important natural tool you can use to beat anxiety is regular exercise. It sounds cliché, but the truth is that exercise affects the mind and body in ways that science is still discovering.

There is a reason that anxiety prevalence has grown with our increasingly inactive lifestyles. Jogging every day can make a world of difference in how you deal with stress, how your anxiety symptoms manifest, and how you regulate your mood.

The best methods of exercise to combat anxiety are:

- **Running** releases feel-good hormones that have exponential mental health benefits. It can help you fall asleep faster, improve memory, lower stress levels, and protects against developing depression.

- **Hiking** in a wooded or hilly location has natural calming effects on the brain. Being around plants and Earthly sights helps to reduce anxiety thanks to the chemicals plants emit. Plus, being out in nature is great for your health and memory function.

- **Yoga,** a lot like meditation, has been found to significantly reduce anxiety and other neurotic symptoms that can lead to irritability and depression. It not only strengthens your core but helps you to focus on breathing, which is the key to relaxing the mind and combating anxiety.

Chapter 9: Rediscovering yourself after hurricane anxiety

Those that live with and through the darkness of anxiety can find themselves waking up each day unhappy. Life is short and there comes a time where re-evaluating your life in order to revamp parts of it to ensure your happiness and fulfillment.

We all get lost in life from time to time. We forget old passions we had, give up interest in pursuit of something else, etc. But it is never too late to rediscover what makes you great and what makes you feel truly alive.

When were you the *happiest*?

Take a moment to remember when you were the most content with your life. In high school? College? Before marriage, family, and kids? When you began your family? Started your business? Pursued a new hobby?

No one peaks at the same time or levels in their lives. The key to regaining contentment is not to think of those fond times as "the past", but to figure out how to find that feeling of happiness again where you currently are in your life. How can you re-incorporate those things that brought you joy in the life you are living now?

What makes you *unhappy*?

What makes your blood pressure shoot through the roof? Figuring out the things that push your last buttons is just as important as knowing what helps you keep a positive outlook. When you are able to clearly point out the toxic influences, you will be better able to erase them and develop better, healthier ways of living. We tend to hold onto things from the past that has negative impacts on our current lives. What grudges are you holding onto? These are toxic and are keeping you from being your best self! No matter what it is, from a toxic ex-partner to a job that drains you, cutting these negative influences will allow you ample space to grow in a positive direction.

Write!

When negative thoughts are constantly bouncing around the brain, it can be very easy to become overwhelmed. We tend to forget how much our daily thoughts impact our lives. They take hold of our power, telling us who we are and what are and aren't capable of. We are the only ones that have the power to take action to erase pesky thoughts from inhibiting our success in life.

I have found that organizing thoughts by writing them down makes them more abstract. When you can visualize them on paper, it makes them concrete.

Write out a list of pros and cons, random thoughts that pop up, poetry, grocery lists, anything that comes to mind. All writing can be therapeutic and helps us to rediscover how our voice sounds, which radiates who. I challenge to find yourself again with the power of good old pen and paper.

Learning to Love Yourself Again

To rediscover yourself, you need to learn how to love yourself again for who you are, and all parts of yourself, including your flaws and everything you have endured. There are millions of places that offer up 'good advice' to practice self-love, but they never explain exactly how to do so.

Loving yourself is a vital piece of the puzzle when it comes to positive personal growth. It allows us to fulfill our dreams and create happy and healthy relationships with others too.

Care about yourself as much as you care about others

This sounds almost too simple, but many of us are not selfish enough when it comes to fulfilling our wants and needs. It is hard to remember that you are **not** selfish when it comes to caring about yourself and your wellbeing.

Showing yourself compassion shows those in your life that you are able to take care of yourself. No one can pour from an empty pot, which means you need to take care of yourself in order to take care of others in your life. Treat yourself the way you treat your best friend, with caring, concern, and gentleness, no matter what is happening in your life.

Maintain boundaries

Jot down a list of things you need emotionally, both what is important to you and what upsets you. The list can be made up of anything, from wanting sympathy to being celebrated, to being cared for, etc. Whatever is important to you, no matter how silly it sounds, **Write. It. Down.**

We can often find ourselves smack dab in the middle of the confusing conflict and wonder how we got there in the first place. We ask ourselves how we attracted this situation and the people in it with us. While you still need to take responsibility for your actions, it is also crucial to not fall into a pit of self-blame that can cause stress, but rather really look into what is occurring. Many people lack inner confidence and have no idea what they are worth. This lack can leave us living in a sum-zero equation; we are loved completely or become completely unlovable.

I have found from my psychological studies and personal experiences that there are two very simple questions to help anyone restore healthy boundaries in their life to live a dignified life:

What does this situation negatively represent about yourself? How are you tolerating situations and the behaviors of those around you reinforces your low-worth within you? Those in our lives are a mirror of our own biases, hopes, and fears. *"All anger stems from anger at the self."*

What is your worst fear about saying "no"? Have you ever been left with the thought of you are a bad person because someone's behavior has left you feeling guilty? Well, stop! Challenge that thought by thinking about other situations you have been through. When that happens, the thought that you are a "bad person" falls apart. What matters, in the end, is simple math: people will either *add* or *subtract* to your life.

So, what have you written? The things you write are what you should consider your personal boundaries. When someone ignores something on that list, you should consider it as them crossing boundaries that you have respectively set for yourself. Do not ignore how you feel if this happens, for they are there to tell you what is right from wrong.

Inform others about the boundaries you have set for yourself and be forthcoming with what you will and will not tolerate. When you are assertive with your boundaries, this plays an important part in building a positive self-esteem and allows you many opportunities to reinforce your beliefs, what you cherish, and what you deserve from life.

Do YOU?

Take the time for yourself to establish the things that make you feel good about yourself and about your life as a whole, no matter what it is. Just learn to be aware of how you feel when you go about acting on certain things. For example:

- Are you exhausted by the work you do, but feel thrilled when gardening?
- Are you joyful when reading out loud to your children?
- Do you feel a sense of fulfillment when you write poetry or volunteer in your community?

Once you figure out what makes you feel good about yourself, make those things a priority by implementing them into your every day or weekly schedule. No matter what makes sure you go out and do them! This may mean you have to give up other things to make time for them, but it also means that you may need to re-evaluate your schedule and life more so that you are doing what you honestly enjoy.

To ensure that you are doing these things, there are more than likely going to have to be actions you take to get to those happiness goals, such as saving money to buy supplies to paint, waking up an hour earlier, exercising more, etc.

It is important to realize that you need to do what you need to in order to fulfill your happiness goals. You cannot allow yourself to blame others if you do not fulfill these things. It is time to be a little selfish and fill up your own teapot so that you can fill up the cups of others in your life! This will help you to not only feel better and do better by other people, but it will help you to clear the fog on inconsistent negativity from your life and enable you to truly love yourself and your life once more.

PART II

Chapter 1: Why So Sensitive?

"For a highly sensitive person, a drizzle feels like a monsoon."

-Anonymous

When something out of the ordinary happens, and it is relatively minor, you may become a little surprised, sad, anxious, or happy, depending on what the situation is. Even though the event happened out of nowhere, it elicits a minor emotional response. This will be the case if your emotional reactions are that of a normal individual. However, if you are part of the subset of the population which is highly sensitive, then your response will be anything but minor.

Imagine going completely over the top with your feelings when something out of the ordinary happens in your life. If you go through a distraught situation, you become much more saddened than those around you. If a friend has something good happen to them, you will act more excited than they do. When someone is loud, you feel it to your core. If this sounds like you, then you might be a highly sensitive person.

Individuals who are highly sensitive display stronger reactivity to external and internal stimuli, whether emotional, physical, or social. They are thought to have deeper sensitivities at the central nervous system. It is estimated that about 15-20 percent of the population falls under this umbrella. Highly sensitive persons are believed to be much more disturbed by violence or tension. If they see something bad happen on the news, they will be distraught and might even be bothered by it the whole day. In contrast, someone who is not in their shoes will just think about it for a moment. On the flip side, if you make them happy, they will be exceptionally excited beyond control. It's how they are built.

This may not sound like a big deal to most. You have probably known several people who are overly emotional. However, this goes beyond just crying a little extra during a movie. If you were to go inside the mind of a highly sensitive person, what you are likely to experience would overwhelm you instantly. If you are living with this mindset, then you know exactly what I am talking about.

Despite what people may think, highly sensitive people are not dramatic for no reason. They often cannot help the way they react in certain situations. At least, not without becoming aware of it first. These individuals will often notice things much more acutely than other people do. This relates especially to the feelings of others. While most individuals will simply overlook the pain and suffering of someone else, a highly sensitive person will be more aware of their emotions. They may not know exactly what is wrong, but just that something is okay. They will pick up on the subtleties of body language, facial expressions, and tone of voice. Even if they don't know an individual, they will be in-tune with the vibes the person puts off. All sensitivity radars will be off the charts.

How To Tell If You're In The Camp

If you have always felt a little different than everybody else around you, then you might be dealing with a highly sensitive personality. Of course, there are many different attributes to consider before knowing for sure. The following are some of the signs of being in this camp. Once you understand whether you're a highly sensitive person or not, then we can proceed forward.

- You are extremely unsettled by cruelty or violence. While most people don't enjoy violence, a highly sensitive person will become extremely disturbed or physically ill by it, even if they don't see it personally.
- You are frequently emotionally exhausted because of how others feel. Essentially, other people and their feelings have a deep impact on you.
- Time crunches make you extremely anxious and overwhelmed. While approaching deadlines can make anyone's hair get raised, it is exponentially greater for a highly sensitive person.
- You enjoy going int solitude at the end of the day to reduce your stimulation levels.
- You are very jumpy and become frightened quickly.
- You are a very deep thinker. You often reflect on your life and experiences to process everything. You will also play events in your head over and over again.
- You seek to find answers to life's questions and wonder why things are the way they are.
- You are startled easily by sudden, loud noises.
- You have reduced pain tolerance.

- You have a rich inner world. You probably grew up with many imaginary friends and might still have them as an adult. You frequently go into a fantasy world.

- You are extremely upset by change, whether positive or negative. It can really throw you off.

- You are very sensitive to the environmental stimuli around you, like the birds chirping, sirens, new smells, or unusual sites. This is because all of your senses are heightened.

- When you're hungry, you become angry too.

- You hate conflict and disagreements. You want people to get along and not fight with each other. You definitely avoid confrontation if you can.

- You are very thin-skinned. You do not take criticism well, whether it is constructive or not.

- You're very conscientious of making mistakes. You're not perfect, but you try extremely hard to be.

- The beauty of your surroundings moves you deeply. Whether it is artwork, a rich scent, or a delicious looking meal, you are enthralled by all of it.

- You will compare yourself to others and often feel inferior as a result.

- You are very perceptive and insightful. You pick up on things that others don't.

If you have been dealing with the issue of being highly sensitive, then you have probably been looked down upon your whole life. People may have told you to toughen up, be less sensitive, or grow a backbone. Don't take any of these statements personally because these individuals did not know better. In fact, you may not have known better and thought there was something wrong with you. Well, as you read further, you will actually begin to understand your unique gifts.

What Makes People Overly Sensitive?

There are many factors to consider when deciding on why you are a highly sensitive person. If having these feelings is an anomaly for you, meaning it's not your normal personality, then it is probably a unique life event that is causing you to behave in this manner. For example, losing a loved one, having poor health, not eating properly, or getting a lack of sleep may contribute to feelings of over sensitivity. However, if you have always been this way, then it goes well-beyond life events. It is ingrained in you to be a highly sensitive person.

Children who were severely criticized, bullied, or went through some type of abuse or trauma can also end up being highly sensitive. Their psyches took a major hit while they were children, so they grew up to be unsure of themselves, which may have contributed to their over-sensitivity, as a result.

Your highly sensitive feelings are likely to have a genetic component to them. So, you might have been born this way as it was passed on through your genes. Also, environmental and social factors may be involved. If your parents, or those you grew up around, were highly sensitive people, then you might have picked up on their personality traits and acquired them as your own. Of course, you can also end up completely opposite from your parents and other influential people, so their attributes may not mean anything in relation to you.

Overall, a highly sensitive person is thought to have a brain that is wired differently, so it has a lower threshold for the environment. So, any type of stimulus will have an exponential effect on them. Many of these characteristics can be seen in babies, as some infants are much more emotional and sensitive to things like sound. This further suggests that people are born highly sensitive, rather than made. In the mid-1990s, husband and wife psychology duo, Arthur and Elaine Aron, coined the term "sensory-processing sensitivity," which is the official scientific phrase used to describe a highly sensitive person. Through their research, the husband and wife duo stated further that the nervous system of someone with sensory-processing sensitivity had variations in their nervous system that was different from others who did not display highly sensitive qualities.

Negative Aspects Of Being A Highly Sensitive Person

Being in the camp of high sensitivity can certainly have their advantages, which we will go over in the next chapter. For now, I will discuss the negative aspects of being a highly sensitive person. This personality trait can impact every area of your life, and if you are not careful, it can create a lot of pain and suffering in the long run. Unfortunately, people will take advantage of the kind qualities of a sensitive individual, and the results are not always pleasant.

In The Workplace

If you are like the majority of people in the world, then you probably spend much of your time in the workplace. Here, you will have regular interactions with your coworkers and those in upper management. While certain things in the workplace may be a slight struggle or annoyance for most individuals, a highly sensitive person may have their whole workflow and mood affected in a significant way. The following are certain obstacles that only a highly sensitive person would understand and contend within the workplace.

- A strong aroma in the office can completely throw off a highly sensitive person. These can be smells that come from different foods or from someone wearing a lot of perfume.

- Other sensory issues like bright colors or loud sounds in the workspace, can severely affect their focus and ability to do their job.

- Trying to complete last-minute deadlines without proper planning can cause a highly sensitive person to become overwhelmed quickly. This is definitely not when they do their best work.

- Criticism from a boss or employee can truly mess with a highly sensitive person's head. They may even react in an unorthodox fashion, like having a mental breakdown, crying excessively, or running out of the office. They often cannot help it as it is an instantaneous reaction.

- Highly sensitive people will have a hard time speaking up and asking for what they want or need. They hate rocking the boat and definitely don't want to upset anyone else. As a result, they are often overlooked for many opportunities.

- These individuals are often seen as weak and ineffectual, so people will walk all over them. The highly sensitive person will usually let them.

- They are usually overstressed, even if it's a normal workday with nothing unusual going on. Anything in their environment can make them feel this way. Remember that highly sensitive people are more prone to be affected by environmental stimuli.

- There will be constant comparison with coworkers, and the highly sensitive person will always feel like they come up short.

- Wearing professional clothes, like ties, high-heels, or various other things that are uncomfortable, are highly bothersome to you.

As a highly sensitive person, you must be aware of these unique traits and how they will make you react. Otherwise, your experience at work will become constant suffrage.

In Their Personal Lives

Highly sensitive people will also deal with others in their personal lives, both at home and in various relationships. Their personality traits will often not do them any favors in this aspect of their lives, either. As a highly sensitive person, you will have extremely emotional and sometimes hostile relationships with those close to you. The following are some issues you may run into.

- Highly sensitive people will sense when their friends and family are going through some issues. They will also allow these emotions to overwhelm them.
- If a highly sensitive person gets asked to do something, in most cases, they will say yes, no matter how busy their schedule is or what they have planned. Saying no is a true challenge.
- These individuals are their own worst critic and will be excessively hard on themselves for something, while easily forgiving someone else for the same issues.
- They are often poor with self-care because they are too busy worrying about others.
- They are more sensitive to trouble and conflict within a relationship. They will become stressed easily during a conflict.
- They will have a lot of self-doubt about their abilities, which will show in their personal relationships. They will usually be the ones to submit and compromise full.

- They will have a hard time asking their friends for anything.
- It will be very easy to hurt a highly sensitive person's feelings. Plus, they can be manipulated easily.

As you can see, a highly sensitive person will not have an easy time with their personal relationships. They will usually be the givers and never the takers. These qualities can wear down on them and create much emotional and psychological harm if not dealt with accordingly.

Now that we have a picture of what a highly sensitive person is, you probably have a pretty good idea if you are one or not. We will get into more detail about the positive qualities of this personality trait.

Chapter 2: Embrace Your Sensitivities

I know I was pretty hard on highly sensitive people in chapter one and did not paint them in the most positive light. It is hard to imagine that these individuals actually have positive qualities. However, just because a highly sensitive person has flaws and weaknesses does not mean they don't have significant strengths too. In this section, I will go over the reasons why being a highly sensitive person is a good thing and how people can start embracing this aspect of themselves.

Benefits Of Being a Highly Sensitive Person

There are actually many great qualities to being a highly sensitive person, and the world is lucky to have individuals like this. Sensitivity is falsely depicted as being undesirable, which you have probably noticed in your own life. I am here to tell you that it is not a negative trait to have. With all of the controversy surrounding it, the benefits are often overlooked. But, they cannot be ignored any longer.

Having A Depth Of Experience And Feelings

Experiencing the world with heightened emotions gives you a deeper meaning in everything around you. You learn to find joy in the smallest things, which means you have the ability to find good in every area of life. You learn to experience life in a totally different way as a highly sensitive person and notice beauty in the subtleties of life.

Self-Awareness

Self-awareness means having a strong sense of who you are and where you belong in the world. A highly sensitive person has a keen self-awareness. They are hyper tuned in to their emotions, and the reactions that follow them. While a highly sensitive person understands their high levels of emotional volatility, they eventually realize that other people do not process feelings in the same manner that they do. What throws their minds for a loop, will barely be a blip on the radar for someone else.

Intuitive Nurturing Skills

The highly sensitive person is naturally good at nurturing others. Because of their ability to feel deeply, they have a strong desire to bring happiness to other people. They have the instinct to care for others and will support them, so they feel loved and appreciated.

A Knack For Forming Close relationships

Highly sensitive people may take a while to open up to somebody, but once they do, they form strong bonds in the process. They will become the best companions a person can have. The reason highly sensitive people are choosy with making friends is because they can feel the energy of others around them. If the energies don't mesh, they know the relationships won't be a good fit.

Highly sensitive people are not interested in casual acquaintances, but in developing meaningful relationships. They want to be around individuals who make them feel comfortable.

Appreciating The Small Things In Life

Highly sensitive people are also highly sensitive to things that bring them joy. This means they can find joy in even the smallest things in life. If they are having a bad day, hearing a good song on the radio can completely change their mood.

Why Highly Sensitive People Make Great Friends

As we move through life, we meet and develop relationships with many different people. While we get along and also get to know these individuals well, how many of them truly become great friends? It is rare to find friends who understand us for who we are, leave us feeling warm and make us believe that we are important. A highly sensitive person is a friend who has all of these abilities. These individuals become the best kinds of friends because of the attributes they possess. The following are a few reasons why a highly sensitive person should be a sought-after relationship in your life.

- They are able to manage conflicts well because they have the ability to observe and quickly diffuse a situation. Plus, they have a keen eye for details and can often sense a conflict erupting before it starts.
- They highly understand the needs of others and will work hard to keep their friends happy, including you.
- They like to involve others and help them grow. Even when you make a mistake, they will help you learn from it and maintain your confidence.
- They are not stuck in their own worlds.
- They have a sense of purpose and want to make a difference in people's lives.

If you are a highly sensitive person, know that you can be a great and valuable friend to many people out there.

Why Highly Sensitive People Make Great Employees

While highly sensitive people can struggle in major ways in many work environments, they actually make great employees. The attributes they have make them reliable, hardworking, intuitive, and great team players. Rarely will they cause drama. In fact, they will do their best to avoid it.

Highly sensitive people are often undervalued in the workplace. They are not the most charismatic or outspoken people in the office. In fact, they are probably the ones you will hear from the least. Unfortunately, the soft skills they bring to the table do not get the same recognition as the stronger skills. This does not mean they are less valuable as employees, though. The following are some of the reasons highly sensitive people are a great addition to any company.

- They are the ones you can count on. They have the right attitude, will always show up, and will put in the effort needed to get the job done.
- They are careful decision-makers and will rarely take action hastily. As a result, the decisions they make are often the best possible under the circumstances at the moment.
- If they are in a positive environment, they will thrive beyond your imagination.
- They can be creative and, therefore, find the right solutions to problems.
- People often think that leaders have to be loud and brash. Actually, this is the opposite of what a leader should be. True leaders are intuitive,

listen well, and inspire others. This is why a highly sensitive person actually makes a great leader.

- Highly sensitive people will focus on what benefits the team, rather than what benefits themselves.

If you are a highly sensitive person, know that your attributes are truly desired in the workplace, even if it doesn't seem that way.

Guess what? As a highly sensitive person, you are special and bring a unique gift to this world. Too many people are stuck in their own heads and have no concept or understanding of the world around them. You, on the other hand, can acknowledge the thoughts and feelings of other people. Because of your great attributes, you must stop believing that you are undesirable or weak. You are actually the strong one. The next chapter will discuss how you can start believing in yourself and the value that you bring to the world. You will become a better person overall.

Chapter 3: Living As A Highly Sensitive Person

The key to living a happy life as a highly sensitive person is to embrace the good qualities that you possess and showcase them to the world, while not allowing your flaws to control you. The bad part about highly sensitive people is that their oversensitivity gets the best of them, and often at the most inopportune times. The goal of this chapter will be to focus on controlling your emotions and allowing your unique gifts to shine through by using specific action steps to rewire your brain and way of thinking. Mindset shifts will be a major factor in managing your habits and sensitivities. Once you go through the practices and action steps I discuss here; you will truly be able to live your best life as a highly sensitive person.

The first step in the process is realizing who you are. In the previous two chapters, I detailed the positive and negative attributes of a highly sensitive person. In the end, while having this trait has extreme downsides, the positives outweigh the negatives. If you have come to realize that you are a highly sensitive person, then it's time to move on to the strategies and actions steps to manage your emotions.

How To Overcome Your Sensitivities

Just to be clear, you will never get rid of your sensitivities. They have always been a part of who and always will be. The objective is to manage these sensitivities, so you can overcome them. If they control you, they can become a major obstacle. The key is to use them to your advantage by controlling them. The following are some survival tips for highly sensitive people so that they don't become overwhelmed.

- Get plenty of sleep. Usually, 7-8 hours is recommended, but whatever it takes t make you feel well-rested. A lack of sleep will make you irritable, moody, less productive, and decrease your concentration. Proper sleep will help soothe your senses.

- Eat healthy food throughout the day. People dismiss how much of an effect diet has on your mood. But, if you eat foods high in cholesterol, saturated fats, and sugars, you will become tired, irritable, and overly sensitive to stimuli.

- A good pair of headphones can keep you from getting triggered with loud noises. You cannot control the noise, but you can manage how much it affects you.

- Plan time to decompress. Being on the go all the time will always keep you on heightened alert. This means you will continuously be in a frazzled state of mind. Taking time to decompress, preferably at night, can allow your nerves to calm down and no longer be affected by external stimuli. Whatever you can do to isolate yourself from the craziness of the world, do it.

- Give yourself the time and space to get things done. Highly sensitive people do not do well with a packed schedule, so avoid getting yourself in this position if you can help it.

- Limit your caffeine intake. Caffeine is a natural stimulant that will make you feel jittery if taken in excess. Highly sensitive people might be even more sensitive to caffeine. If you drink two cups of coffee a day, cut it down to one.

- Try to avoid excessively lighted areas if you can. In your home, keep your lights dim, as well.

- Get your errands done during the off-hours. This means going out opposite the average person's regular schedule. Get your shopping done during the week, go out with friends on weeknights, and go to the gym early in the morning. The goal here is to avoid huge crowds that can stir up your emotions.

- Get out in nature as much as possible and get away from the hustle-and-bustle of the city.

Even though you are born being highly sensitive, there are still many environmental factors that can trigger you to become more over the top. The survival tips above are meant to prevent overloading your hypersensitive senses. Many psychologists and research scientists have stated that a proper lifestyle may not change our genetics, but it can keep it from making our issues worse.

Having Self-Esteem As A Highly Sensitive Person

Te thing that highly sensitive people struggle with the most is their self-esteem, which is the value and worth they place on themselves. This is because they allow their environment, including the people, around them, to dictate their emotions. It is difficult for these individuals to break away from the feeling other people are having. As a highly sensitive person yourself, it's time for you to start realizing the importance of self-esteem and begin to recognize ways you can improve your own. It is time to stop thinking you are not good enough. The following strategies will take a lot of practice, but once you start implementing them, you will notice major changes in your mindset.

Accept Thoughts, Emotions, And Sensations As They Are

All of these aspects are a part of you but do not define you. They are fleeting in nature and are changing from moment to moment. If you are feeling pain, whether emotional or physical, for a definitive moment, that does not mean you are weak. It is a sensation you are going through that will eventually pass. Instead of letting your thoughts and feeling control you, work on observing them objectively and then letting them go. Do not allow them to become attached to you.

Eliminate The Word "Should" From Your Vocabulary

When you use the word "should," it will elicit a sense of guilt inside of you. If you change it to "could," then you subconsciously open up your mind about what you could be doing and uses less judgment. Using the word "could" also showcases that there are many different options for us, and we are not required to stay on one path. Try it out:

"I should be going to the gym." Change it to, "I could be going to the gym." See the difference?

Do Not Rely On Other People For Self-Esteem

Unfortunately, as highly sensitive people, most of our self-worth is dependent on what other people think of us. You will never place true value on yourself if this is the mindset you will carry. The major problem is that when our outside source for self-esteem vanishes, then the opinion we have of ourselves plummets. We have to internalize our power to create our value and become the sole person who is in charge of it.

Forgive

We all have something in our past that we are not proud of. We must learn to forgive ourselves for the mistakes we made so we can move on. We need to apply the same compassion for ourselves that we tend to show other people. The next time you are hard on yourself, imagine one of your best friends standing in your position. Now, picture what you would tell this person if they made the same mistakes you did. If it's something favorable, then tell yourself the same thing. Stop being your worst critic.

Take Stock Of Your Talents

We tend to focus on our faults, and this severely lowers our self-esteem. We do not give ourselves enough credit by doing this. It is time to take stock of your talents and remember the gifts that you bring to the world. Identify what you are good at. If you are having a tough time coming up with something, then start small. Perhaps you are good at putting things away. This is a good start. As you come up with things, write them down and keep them to look at constantly. Another exercise you can do is write down what you think you're not good at and then crumble up that piece of paper and throw it away. Focus on your positive attributes.

Remember that these exercises will take a lot of consistency. Do not just quit after one day. When you begin incorporating these strategies into your daily life, you will see vast improvements with your mindset.

Focusing On Jobs, You Are Good At

I discussed in the previous chapter about highly sensitive people being model employees. This is still true. However, the goal is to make yourself as happy as possible, and this means avoiding things that will trigger your sensitivities. That being said, there are certain environments and job types where a highly sensitive person will fit in better and even thrive. If you can avoid the stress altogether, then why not do so? The following are the best career options for you if you are a highly sensitive person.

Caring Professions

Careers that require a lot of caring and compassion will be right up a highly sensitive person's alley. These jobs include things like nursing, medicine, counseling, therapy, and coaching. These fields will target a highly sensitive person's strength. Bear in mind that certain areas, like the emergency department or the ICU, may be challenging areas for you. Also, any busy environment will have a lot of different emotions that you will have to contend with. Good options in these fields may be things like home health nursing or individual counseling.

Creative Endeavors

Highly sensitive people are often very creative, so they will thrive in professions where they can show off their creativity. Some of these roles include graphic designer, writer, photographer, artist, or architect. Many creative jobs can be done on a freelance basis, which allows you to create your own schedule. This will be a major benefit to you as a highly sensitive person.

Clergy

If you have a spiritual side to you, then working as a clergy person may be right for you. Bear in mind, that depending on the denomination, you may have to follow strict rules. This may cause difficulty if you are a highly open-minded person. Of course, if you can get over the structure, then your intuition and sensitivity will be valued and accepted.

Academia

With academia, you get to spend a significant amount of time doing thoughtful and intensive research on a subject you have an interest in. In addition, you get to teach your extensive knowledge to students; as a highly sensitive person, you will thrive in your areas. In the end, you are doing meaningful work throughout your profession.

IT Professional

Coding is a major portion of IT and requires a lot of creativity to be successful. You will also need strong intuition and an eye for detail. These are all qualities that are possessed by highly sensitive people. As one of these individuals, software engineering or website development might be the perfect career paths for you.

When choosing a career to go into, you should focus on your strengths and what areas you will be compatible with. Consider your strengths as a highly sensitive person and determine what line of work fits you best.

Dealing With Hyperarousal

There will be times when you are in a state of hyperarousal, where you will be wired up and out of control, physically and mentally. In some cases, hyperarousal can be a defense mechanism, like with the fight-or-flight response. In these moments, being on high alert is a necessity. However, when the hyperarousal goes beyond defined moments, you will be dealing with many problems, including stress, anxiety, and overall diminished emotional and physical health. Yes, being in a state of constant arousal is detrimental to your physical health. Prolonged stress has led to many chronic illnesses, like heart disease, stroke, diabetes, and even some cancers. In addition, mental health disorders like depression are also a possibility.

When you are in the hyperarousal state, you will have an increased heart rate, faster breathing, quicker reflexes, perspiration, and heightened sensitivity to stimuli. So, when you hear a loud noise, you will immediately jump into action, or at least be ready to. Once again, short-term physiological responses like these are not dangerous. If you are consistently in this state, then we have a problem that must be addressed.

Hyperarousal needs to be dealt with quickly; otherwise, it will take over your life. This response is a symptom of another problem, so if you can figure out that problem is, then you can address it directly. The following are some action steps that will have a favorable response to being wired.

Practice Mindfulness

The purpose of this technique is to sit peacefully and consciously observe the chaos and frantic thoughts going on inside your mind without trying to change them, escape from them, or fight them off. Many therapists use this technique with their clients because it is effective in getting over feelings of panic. It also helps to reduce your hyperarousal symptoms.

Perform this technique for about 1-5 minutes at a time. Just sit quietly and focus on your feelings of discomfort, agitation, and anxiety. Concentrate very hard in this area. See if you can visualize these negative feelings and imagine holding them in your arms. A common practice that therapists have their clients do is picture the problems they are holding as being much bigger and worse. It may sound confusing, but it works well for their clients. It is likely because once they've imagined the issue being worse, the thing does not seem as major.

Make Small Achievable Goals Towards Relaxation And Calmness

I do mean to make these goals achievable by keeping them small. When you first start out, shoot for 30 seconds of pure relaxations. Once you achieve this milestone, then try for one minute, then two minutes, and so on. Eventually, you will be able to be in this state for several minutes with no problems. Just work your way up.

It does not matter what relaxation techniques you use, as long as you are in a state of physical relaxation and calmness. This can mean lying down in bed, sitting in a comfortable chair, or meditating. The choice is yours. From here, remain quiet and focus on a body part that feels tense. Now, take one breath in slowly over a few seconds, then hold it for a few seconds before letting it out slowly. As you release the breath, imagine the tension leaving that part of the body you focused on earlier. Truly visualize the tension dissipating like a cloud of smoke.

Evaluate yourself after this. Did your breathing and pulse rate decrease? Do you feel less tense and anxious? If so, then the practice was a success. Keep working on this step to make yourself better.

Positive Self-Talk

In the middle of frantic self-talk that is negative, interrupt yourself and begin saying some encouraging phrases. These include statements like, "You will get through this," or "You are strong and will overcome." This technique will trick your mind and shift it from positive to negative. As a result, you will slow down your pace. Once you do this often, it will become a habit.

Investigate The Root Cause

The above exercises are beneficial; however, you should also determine what the root cause of your hyperarousal is. If you can figure this out, then the risk of flareups in the future will go down. Some of the causes include anxiety, PTSD, excess caffeine, and drug or alcohol use. Once you've narrowed it down, then you can focus on more specific techniques to eliminate the root cause.

For example, Cognitive Behavioral Therapy, or CBT, can be an effective strategy from anxiety. The goal of CBT is to challenge your current thought patterns through talk therapy. The following are a few key steps to make CBT work for you.

- Identify what you are thinking by actually writing them down on something. This way, you can visualize them.
- Assess your thoughts and realize that they may not be true or accurate. We often think negative thoughts for so long that we automatically assume they identify us, and we never challenge them.
- Replace these harmful thoughts with more positive and encouraging ones. Write down all of these new thoughts, as well.
- Now, read these new thoughts to yourself over and over again. Do this until it becomes a habit for you to think of these thoughts, which could take days or weeks.

CBT is a strategy that works for many different disorders, and therapists use it often.

The bottom line to all of this is that you will always be a highly sensitive person. It is not something you can avoid, nor should you try to do so. Despite the challenges that may exist, being a highly sensitive person is still a unique gift that you should embrace every day. Learning the techniques to control your thoughts and emotions, and not allowing your environment to overwhelm, you will ensure that you live a happy and satisfying life. Your sensitivity and intuitiveness are a true gift for many people.

PART III

Chapter 1: Understanding Panic Attacks and Panic Disorders

Imagine the fear of watching a giant wave coming roaring towards you, while you stand frozen, unable to move an inch.

It is frightening. Have you ever experienced any such fear?
Imagine having extreme breathing difficulty all of a sudden, like having an asthma attack, without suffering from asthma.

It's scary and suffocating. Have you been in any such situation ever?
Imagine being in a situation when you are quite sure that you are not going to survive that crisis; only there is no such crisis.

It is a terrible experience. Have you been through it?
These are real-life situations that a panic attack might look like. To an onlooker, a panic may look like an overreaction. Most people consider panic attacks as dodging tactics using which you can escape facing tough situations. However, they are unable to understand that during a panic attack, the victim experiences difficulty in breathing, the actual feeling of an allergic reaction is there.

For many victims, there is a feeling of the throat closing up, feels like throat tightening, and it seems like a reaction of a body as if you were about to die, nausea, heart palpitation, excessive sweating, blackouts, chest pain, and complete loss of control are some of the common symptoms panic attack victims may experience during the attacks.

Panic attacks can come out of the blue without a prior warning or even without triggers. They are scarier than they sound because the panic attack victim can feel them approaching because there's nowhere to run. The warning signal is coming from the inside, and you can't run away from yourself.

Many people start saying breathe deeply, relax, or be calm, but all these suggestions are useless because the words don't reach the effective areas. Deep breathing can help the victim relax and avoid panic attacks, but that advice and assurance must come from inside. The realization that you can avert the attack by simply diverting your mind and staying calm must be there in you. There is no doubt that a panic attack victim would have to work on developing this confidence and realization, but it is very much possible.

What Is a Panic Attack?

Excessive anxieties and fears can lead to panic attacks. During a panic attack, the victim can experience several symptoms like racing heart, heart palpitation, excessive shaking, breathing difficulties, and nausea. Things simply start slipping out of control, and the victim starts feeling very helpless and vulnerable. Every panic attack victim doesn't experience all the symptoms mentioned above. As per the Diagnostic and Statistical Manual of Mental Disorders, fourth edition, if a victim experiences any of the four symptoms from the list given below, the victim is considered to have experienced a panic attack.

The real tell-tale sign of a panic attack is that it builds up rapidly. A person could be doing fine just a few minutes ago, and all of a sudden can start exhibiting signs of fear, anxiety, pain, and discomfort. A panic attack generally reaches its peak within ten minutes of the beginning.

Important Symptoms, the Victim of a Panic Attack, Is Likely to Experience:

(A person experiencing at least four of the symptoms at the same time is classified as experiencing a panic attack.)

1. Sensations of shortness of breath or smothering
2. Palpitations, pounding heart, or accelerated rate of heart
3. Trembling or shaking
4. Feeling lightheaded, unsteady, dizzy, or faint
5. Fear of losing control or going crazy
6. Chills or hot flushes
7. Sweating
8. Feeling of choking
9. Discomfort or chest pain
10. Nausea or abdominal distress
11. Fear of dying

12. Paresthesias (tingling sensations or numbness)
13. Derealization (a sense of unreality) or depersonalization (feeling detached from oneself)

As mentioned above, panic attacks symptoms appear very fast and do not allow the victim to understand much. It can peak within a short span of just 10 minutes, and hence initially, the victims generally do not get a chance to react properly.

A panic attack can make the victim feel like he/she isn't going to survive it. To some, the acute chest pain looks like a heart attack, and to others, the breathing difficulty episodes brought by panic attacks resemble asthma attacks. Most victims end up in emergency rooms only to be told later on that they had a panic attack.

It is important to understand that panic attacks don't last very long. A panic attack can begin out of the blue without a trigger and may reach its peak within 10 minutes. However, in most cases, panic attacks get resolved within half an hour. It is rare for a panic attack to last an hour.

Although panic attacks may last only for half an hour, for the victim, this duration may seem like an eternity. The whole period is physically and emotionally very stressful and overwhelming. It is the extreme stress experienced during the panic attack that may make it feel like a very long period, and it can be emotionally churning.

It is very important to note that there is no specific cause of panic attacks. Panic attacks can be caused by various stressors, and the genetic buildup of a person can make a person prone to panic attacks. However, people with mood disorders and long-standing anxiety issues are naturally soft-targets of panic attacks. Severe stress, major transitions in life, a feeling of acute vulnerability, and several medical conditions can also make a person prone to panic attacks.

What Is Panic Disorder and Should You Be Worried About It?

Panic disorder is having an extended fear of panic attacks all the time, even when you haven't had a panic attack in a month or more.

It is very much possible for a person to just have one or two episodes of panic attacks and then never have them ever. You were passing through a bad patch in life that made you insecure and vulnerable and caused a panic attack. When then phase passes away, you might not experience a panic attack ever again. Unfortunately, some people experience repeated panic attacks, and they undergo substantial behavioral changes making anxiety a part of their lives. They are always anxious about the next attack to come. Such people can be termed as suffering from **Panic Disorder**.

Symptoms That a Person Might be Developing Panic Disorder are:

- Constant worry about panic attacks
- Frequent episodes of panic attacks out of the blue
- Clear avoidance of things and situations that might have led to a panic attack

Panic disorders are the quiet periods between panic attacks, and they can be more harmful than panic attacks as they can severely affect the life and functioning of the victim. They can be as threatening as the silence before a storm, and that's what keeps the victims on edge.

Emotionally, panic disorder can take a toll on the mental health of the victim as it keeps the mind full of fearful thoughts and anxieties. Finding a diversion can get difficult in such a condition. The victims are unable to push the fear of an attack from their mind, and they are always in fear of an impending attack.

Chapter 2: Anxiety and Panic Attacks Aren't the Same

There are many common symptoms in anxiety and panic attacks, and that makes people draw a misleading conclusion that having anxiety disorders and panic attacks or panic disorders is all the same.

Very Important

You must make it very clear in your mind that having a panic attack is an easily treatable condition. If you've just had a few episodes of panic attacks, you can just go to a doctor and get treatment for that. A simple medication routine of a fortnight can help you get over panic attacks. However, treatment of anxiety disorders is a very lengthy process that may take years while using both medication and therapy.

Therefore, if you or someone you know just had a panic attack, there is no reason to worry as it is a treatable condition.

Differentiating between both the conditions can be a bit tricky and may need professional help.

However, here are some broad points that can help you understand the difference:

- Anxieties are generally very specific. There are triggers for anxiety. You know the things that can make you feel anxious. There would be specific stressors and triggers that can trigger anxiety in you. On the other hand, panic attacks usually come without a trigger.

- A big difference between anxiety and panic is the way you feel them. Panic attacks are sudden and intense. A panic attack can start all of a sudden without a trigger and would reach its peak in a short span of 10 minutes. Although they are fast and intense and the entire duration of a panic attack may seem like an eternity, usually they don't last longer than half an hour and would rarely extend for an hour. Whereas anxiety can keep building for months.

- Initially, the anxiety would be less, and it can keep intensifying over a long period. As time passes, your anxiety would keep getting stronger, and it simply doesn't pass away like a panic attack.

- Anxieties are usually followed by a long period of worries. It keeps the mind occupied and leads to overthinking and development of deep fear. Panic attacks end fast, and you will feel all the pressure and fear melting away. You'd feel the intense weight being lifted from your head.

Generalized anxiety in this way is much more dangerous and complex than sporadic episodes of panic attacks. It can last for anywhere between a few minutes to your whole lifetime.

However, every fear and anxiety is not bad. Generally, we feel anxious about things we are not comfortable with. When we are anxious, there can be a rapid pounding of heart, increased pulse, sweating, and tension. You get a general feeling of your inability to cope with a certain situation, and hence defensive mechanism gets activated. Most of the time, people choose to avoid things and situations that may cause anxieties. But, that's not possible in the case of panic attacks as they can come without any such trigger or stressor.

Anxiety disorders should never be ignored as they form the basis of several complicated conditions like social anxiety disorder (SAD), obsessive-compulsive disorder (OCD), posttraumatic stress disorder (PTSD), generalized anxiety disorder (GAD), etc.

Chapter 3: Biological and Psychological Causes of Panic Attacks

Biological Causes of Panic Attacks

There is a lot about the brain and its functioning that modern medical science is yet to discover. We know a lot of things, and we are still in the process of finding out a lot more things. The exact physiological causes of panic attacks are also among the few things medical science is trying to find more about.

The science known until now strongly suggests that panic attacks are caused by the faulty alarm system in our brain.

There is an area in the brain known as Locus Ceruleus. This region has a high concentration of adrenaline-like neurons. The impulse conductors of the nerve cells connect this part to:

- The cerebral cortex (the part of the brain determining intelligence, personality, motor function, senses, etc.)
- The limbic system (responsible for our emotions and higher mental function)
- Thalamus (part of the brain managing pain and emotions)
- Hypothalamus (controls the nervous system and hormone signals)

Effectively, any activity in this part of the brain is going to affect your overall functionality.

This locus ceruleus region and the adrenaline-like neurons can stimulate your body to release hormones that can activate a severe 'fight or flight response.'

The body needs this hormone when it is in any kind of danger.

When in danger, the body pumps in adrenaline or epinephrine can make you feel very frightened. In a real-life dangerous situation, that the glucose supply to the cells would be stopped, and all the glucose in the bloodstream would be made available to generate maximum thrust for any action. This simply means that when you are in some grave danger, the power and thrust available to get out of that danger goes up considerably.

This of a scenario where you come face to face with a wild animal. The animal is a quadruped, and hence it has a higher speed than you. In a normal situation, there is no chance for you to outrun that animal. However, due to a very high adrenaline rush in your blood and the resulting fight or flight response, you'll be able to run much faster than your normal capacity to manage survival. This rush is shortlived. It is not possible to manage that speed in normal circumstances, but our body makes a desperate attempt to survive.

This system is there to amplify the chances of survival in dangerous circumstances. Our ancestors had to survive in the wild with no claws, horns, or brute force, whereas the animals were faster, more powerful, and had the accessories like claws, big teeth, and horns. That could make survival difficult, and hence this system was very helpful.

The alarm bells in the locus ceruleus region activate the adrenaline-like neurons, which cause a noradrenergic overload. This is a helpful process in threatening situations. However, in the case of a panic attack, this process gets activated without any stressor or danger trigger. Not only this alarm system gets activated falsely, but it is also very severe in response sending the victim in a state of panic.

Available knowledge and data suggest that this alarm system in our brains is prone to malfunction. Like any alarm system, one or two episodes can occur and then never happen again. This is a reason some people may experience panic attacks once or twice in their lives, never to experience them ever again. Even if you get a panic attack, there is nothing to worry about as just the alarm system has gone off, and otherwise, there is no threat to the body in general. This is a reason panic attacks require no hospitalization or medical care. As there is little understanding of the system, all the causes of the malfunction are not clear, but data shows that hereditary predisposition can make a person prone to such attacks.

There is a high probability that you might have heard the term serotonin. It is commonly used in connection with the things that bring a calming effect to the mind. Instantly after your body has had passed through a severe crisis, you'd notice a feeling of complete relaxation. This feeling of complete relaxation, calm, and peace is brought upon by the effect of serotonin. It is a neuromodulator that helps in modulating anxiety. Gamma-aminobutyric Acid (GABA) is also a neuromodulator chemical. Through several studies, scientists have concluded that when there is a chemical imbalance in the brain, causing low levels of GABA and serotonin, it can lead to panic attacks.

Most theories suggest that the physiological cause of a panic attack somewhere lies in the chemical imbalance in the brain and the faulty alarm system that evokes a crisis response. However, the good thing in these studies is that they suggest this fact with clarity that although the alarm system might be faulty, there is no problem with the basic functioning of the mind and the body.

This means that panic attacks are not a danger for the body. Hence, you don't need to rush to the emergency room every time you have a panic attack or something similar to that. If you could just relax and stay calm, the surge of emotions being experienced by you would pass without an incident.

However, this is easier said than done. The kind of crisis a panic victim feels is only known to that victim. The fear is debilitating. It reduces the victim to nothing. It tears down the personality of the victim. The victims may also face social humiliation due to their sudden reactions. There is no way a panic attack victim can choose the place and time of a panic attack, and that is a reason most victims develop a fear of being in public.

Psychological Causes of Panic Attacks

Panic attacks are strong fear signals being generated in your brain, and your thinking can have a major role to play in that. The kind of temperament you have, the kind of people you socialize with, the kind of job you do, the state of your financial security, etc. are some of the things that can also have a major role in a panic attack.

If any of these things are leading to any kind of insecurity, you can be at risk of a panic attack. You must remember that any kind of major stress in life can lead to a panic attack, and hence leading a balanced life is important.

If you are a person who is sensitive to negative emotions or who cannot handle stressful events, you must work on this aspect of life along with someone who is encouraging and supporting. Fear of things that are very stressful for you can also lead to panic attacks.

Major life events like the demise of a loved one, childhood experience of physical or sexual abuse, or any other such traumatic event recently can also lead to panic attacks.

Abuse of drugs and alcohol can also lead to panic abuse.

Chapter 4: Who Is At a Greater Risk of Panic Attacks?

Anyone can have panic attacks. This is a problem that can strike anyone. Even the marines, who are fitter than the fittest, can suffer from panic attacks. Therefore, if you are fortunate enough to not have experienced any, all you can do is remain cautious. You must remember that even if a panic attack comes, it is a treatable condition.

However, if you fall under any of these categories, you should remain more cautious:

- **Women:** Unfortunately, women have twice the risk of having a panic attack as compared to men. If you are a woman with claustrophobia or any other anxiety disorder, then also your risk of having a panic attack is very high. You'll need to be extra cautious about the things that can cause severe stress.

- **People between 20-29 Age Group:** Although panic attacks can come in any age group, people in the age group of 20-29 years are more likely to experience panic attacks. However, that doesn't mean that people in the younger or older age groups are immune. It can strike at any age.

- **People with a Family History:** As we have already discussed it, if you have someone in your close family with a history of panic attacks or other mental conditions, your risk of having panic attacks can go up.

- **Stressful Life-events:** If you've been through some very stressful life events such as job loss, failure in any big competition, rejection in something crucial, marriage or divorce, or history of abuse, then also the risk of a panic attack will increase.

- **Anxious or Overthinking Attitude:** Some people have anxiety in their attitude. They are never able to feel safe. They always have a lingering fear that something might go wrong. This feeling is even more overpowering when they are sitting at some very pleasant and secure place. It is their mind at play, all the time. Such people are naturally predisposed to panic attacks.

- **Mental Health Illnesses:** If a person has been struggling with generalized anxiety disorder or depression, then the risk of panic attacks will increase.

- **History of Substance Abuse:** Any person with a history of substance abuse will be at a higher risk of panic attacks. Alcohol disorders will also increase the risk many times over.

Chapter 5: Tips to Cope With Panic Attacks When They Strike

You must accept the fact that panic attacks can come. The biggest problem with panic attack victims is that they can't come to terms with the fact that they have panic attacks.

You must realize that you've had a panic attack, and it's okay to have one. You are not the first one and for sure not the last one to have one. Therefore, the best thing to do is to be calm as it is just a phase, and it'd pass away.

Many a time, when someone has a panic attack, the people standing around ask the victim to breathe deeply or be calm and that never really works. It doesn't mean that deep breathing or staying calm are not effective techniques. The victim is simply not in a condition to hear or understand these things. The power to comprehend things said by others during a panic attack goes down. But, if you train your mind and understand the power of deep breathing and other relaxation techniques, you can effectively avoid panic attacks or minimize their severity.

We'll deal with two things in this chapter:

1. Ways to Prevent Panic Attacks
2. Ways to Cope with Panic Attacks

Ways to Prevent Panic Attacks
- **Practice Breathing Exercises:** This is probably one of the most important advice you'll ever hear in panic attack prevention. When having a panic attack, the biggest problem faced is breathlessness. The brain starts getting devoid of oxygen. If you practice deep breathing exercises, you'll be able to prevent panic attacks to a great extent. Breathing exercises are very easy and won't take longer than a few minutes of your time daily. You can practice yoga asanas as they are especially very helpful in preventing panic attacks.

- **Light Exercises**: Exercise has a very positive impact on the brain. When you exercise, the body releases hormones called endorphins that help you in relaxing and also induce a happy mood. Regular exercise can promote a sense of positivity in you and help in preventing panic attacks. However, you must remember that this usually helps when you do light exercises. When you are doing strength training and other accelerated stuff, you must be careful when you are hyperventilating as it can trigger a panic attack. In such a circumstance, your priority must remain to catch your breath first.

- **Manage Blood Sugar Levels:** Keeping your blood sugar levels managed is also a way to prevent panic attacks.

- **Avoid Stimulants like Caffeine, Nicotine, and Alcohol:** Most people know that drug abuse can lead to panic abuse, but a large number of people find it hard to believe that excessive amounts of caffeine, nicotine, and alcohol can also trigger panic attacks. You must try to avoid these.

- **Cognitive Behavioral Therapy (CBT):** This therapy can help you identify and change negative thought patterns leading to panic attacks.

Ways to Cope With Panic Attacks

- **Accept and Recognize:** Panic attacks are short, and they are harmless. You must realize the fact that the episodes you experience don't last long. No matter how bad you might feel at that moment, panic attacks pass, and you are safe again. Therefore, there is no need to fear panic attacks or to stay in denial. If you are having a panic attack, you must recognize it. Once you learn to recognize and accept the fact that you are having a panic attack, it'd be easier to understand that they will pass safely.

- **Deep Breathing:** Breathing deeply while you are having a panic attack is always helpful. Shortness of breath or breathing difficulties are common symptoms of panic attacks, and hence deep breathing will not only help in getting over the panic attacks, but it might even prevent a full-blown panic attack even from happening.

- **Inhale Lavender:** Lavender is a stimulant that can help you feel relaxed. If you get panic attacks frequently, you can keep lavender with you and smell a bit of it when having an attack, and it can help you feel relaxed faster.

- **Medication:** Some medications can help you in coping with panic attacks. If you are having panic attacks frequently, you must consult a doctor and take medication for it.

- **Avoid External Stimuli:** Many a time, loud noise in the background, bright lights, or any other kind of stimuli can also accelerate a panic attack. If you feel a panic attack coming, try to find a peaceful place as it can help you focus inwards, and you'll be able to cope with the panic attack better.

- **Try Meditation Techniques:** Meditation is a great way to train your mind to remain peaceful and calm. It is an effective technique to make your mind avoid fearful thoughts or to divert attention from them. If you can practice meditation for a few minutes daily, you'll be able to overcome the problem of panic attacks to a great extent. There are several meditation forms and techniques that you can try. Some of the effective ones are given below:

o **Mindfulness Meditation:** Most of our panic attacks are either fuelled by our memories of the past or the fears of the future. We are seldom scared of the present as we rarely live in the present. This meditation technique can help you train your mind to live in the present or live mindfully. It can become an effective tool to cope with panic attacks.

o **Diversion of Mind:** During panic attacks, the mind gets focused on a negative thought. If you can focus your attention on a physical point in front of you and meditate only on that point bringing your complete awareness on it, you will be able to prevent or get over the panic attack faster as your mind will get diverted.

o **Muscle Relaxing:** Stiffening of muscles and sensation of pain can also act as a trigger for a panic attack. Practicing progressive-muscle relaxation meditation can help you in relaxing the whole body, and it also takes away the mind from fearful thoughts.

o **Picture a Happy Place:** Guided meditation using imagery of a happy place that you can imagine will also help you in coping better from panic attacks. When your mind is thinking about a happy place, it is very relaxed and calm.

o **Use Positive Affirmation:** You can use positive affirmations during a panic attack to reassure yourself that the panic attack will pass shortly without any incident. Positive affirmations like, 'this is a phase, it'll pass,' or 'you are doing fine, there is nothing to worry' can help you in dealing with the panic attacks better.

Chapter 6: The 8-week Plan to Deal With Panic Attacks

Fighting your fears can be a life-long journey. The fears are not physical; they reside in our minds. The more we think about them, the more intense they get. This chapter would help you understand the ways to tackle the things that have been scaring you for all these years.

The plan has been divided into 8 weeks. 1 week for each plan. During that week, you'll have to work only on that specific issue. You may not be addressing the whole problem, but it'll help you in dealing with the issue in the end.

You must understand that the psychology of fear can be ingrained deep inside your mind, and hence it may take you much longer than 8 weeks too. However, no matter how long it takes, if you follow these 8 steps, you'll be able to get the fear of panic attacks due to specific stressors out of your mind.

Week 1

Identify the Triggers, Fears, and Problematic Behavior
When dealing with any kind of problem, it is very important to understand that problem clearly. The biggest problem with panic attacks lies in the fact that you do not know the things causing them. However, that doesn't mean that you are completely oblivious to your fears. Your panic attack is just a sum-total of your fears. If you can identify and address your fears correctly, you'll be able to get rid of them.

Our fears are not random. They originate from various sections of our lives. We may have a fear of things related to work, education, social interaction, or any specific part of these. Once you identify those fears or triggers, dealing with them would be considerably easy. During the first week, you need to analyze every area in your life and note down the things that may be causing stress, fear, or panic. You should be as detailed as possible in this.

Main Areas of Concern:

Work-Related: Most people feel stressed at work. Although that may not cause a panic attack in every individual, there can be some people who might feel highly stressed at their workplace. You should think of all the things at the workplace that make you feel stressed. Try to be very specific. Like if you feel a sense of panic while being called to give a presentation, you must note it down.

Social Interaction: This is another area where many people feel highly insecure. Some people have anxieties about social interaction, and it can cause a panic attack. You must evaluate if social interactions invoke such a reaction in you. Try to be very specific and focused here. Think of the things that might make you feel nervous. Like if being called to sign in a function makes you feel anxious. Most people will feel nervous in that situation, but do you feel a fight or flight response kicking in?

Health and Well-being: People can get anxious thinking about their health or the health of a family member. Think if you have any fear related to that.

Relationship: Think of your fears related to your existing or past relationships and if they are making you feel anxious.

Other Factors: Think of any other fear that might be lingering deep inside you. There can be many other kinds of fears in mind. Some people are afraid of snakes and scorpions; others are scared of allergies; some are scared of heights. Think of the issue that keeps lingering in your mind.

PinPoint the Issue: You must single out the issue. When you have the problem in view, it is always easy to deal with it. Do not try to limit your entry to any specific thing. List all your fears. Try to know everything that has the potential to make you feel anxious or bring a panic attack.

Week 2

Identify Your Negative Thought Patterns

Once you have the list of things that make you fearful, you can move ahead to deal with the thoughts that lead to such fears. The fears do not come from outside. They are an exaggeration of the thoughts we have about them. Some people may faint when asked to give a speech in front of a gathering while others feel themselves at ease doing so. The task was the same for both, but their minds were working in different ways. The fearful mind started thinking about the consequences of giving that speech like being ridiculed, laughed at, talked about behind the back, saying something unreasonable, etc. The fearless mind saw an opportunity to gain popularity and express views. The situation was the same, but different minds made different assumptions and conclusions. You need to keep in mind that the assumptions made by both could have been wrong. The fearless speakers may have got booed; it happens all the time. However, the fearful speakers would have never reached the podium of completed the speech because the presumptions were incorrect, to begin with.

Our fears are caused by our thoughts, and hence it is important to identify negative thought patterns in the mind to deal with those fears.

Negative thought patterns can be classified in the following broader terms:

> **Unhelpful Thoughts:** These are the thoughts that lead to doubts as you start thinking anything. If you are thinking of undertaking a journey, they'll lead you to think about accidents or bad things that may happen on the journey. If you are thinking of applying for a job, these thoughts will make you think about getting rejected and make you experience that feeling. You must identify if you have unhelpful thoughts very often.

> **What if Thoughts:** These are the thoughts that try to analyze every situation. It may seem logical to think of all the sides of the coin, but it isn't as simple as that. These thoughts will lead you to emphasize on the negative outcomes.

> **Critical Thoughts:** These are the thoughts that make you look at the negative side of everything. You become critical of your abilities, and this can start making you feel insecure, leading to panic attacks.

Victimizing Thoughts: These are the thoughts that make you feel like a victim in every situation. The victim mentality can be very dangerous as it kills all kinds of initiative. It makes you feel exploited and vulnerable, and it can lead to panic attacks. You must identify if you have victimizing thoughts.

Know the Way You Think: To solve any problem, you must know the problem first. Your thoughts are the fuel that leads to the rocket of fear that takes you on panic trips. If you want to avoid panic attacks, it is pertinent that you identify your thought pattern. You must know the way your brain thinks, and then only you will be able to make a strategy to break that thought pattern.

Week 3 and 4

Dissociate From the Negative Thought Patterns

Once the task of identifying negative thought patterns has been completed, you need to devise strategies to change those thought patterns. This may take even longer than two weeks.

Thought patterns develop over a very long period. You may have been practicing the same thought pattern since your childhood. Most thought patterns are picked from the surrounding. This solid conditioning makes the breaking of thought patterns a tough and time-consuming task as you'd need a lot of practice.

However, the only way to do this is to practice it over and over again to make this thought pattern a habit.

Practice Labeling Your Thoughts: This is the first thing that you must do. You learn to label the thought. When you have a negative thought in your mind, learn to label it as 'just a thought.' Our mind is conditioned to consider such thoughts as facts since once it is considered a fact, it is easy to believe. You'll have to identify every negative thought and label it as just a thought, and then it'd be easier to work with it. It wouldn't ring in your brain as the gospel truth.

Make It Funny: If there is any such thought that is making you feel insecure, or which is intimidating you, try to say that out in a funny tone. This simple exercise would help you make light of it. That thought wouldn't remain very fearful or intimidating.

Push Positive Thinking to that Thought: Most negative thoughts become powerful because they never get countered by a positive thought. Try countering the negative thought in your mind with a positive idea.

Evaluate that Thought: You must grade every thought as helpful or unhelpful and discard unhelpful ideas. Once you start grading your thoughts, it'd be easier for you to distance yourself from negative thoughts. They wouldn't have command over your mind.

Find time in the future to ponder over it: If any specific thought is still lingering in your mind, find a time in the future to think it over and get it out of the way. Breaking negative thought patterns should be your focus. If there is any thought that's causing trouble in your mind, either counter it positively or get it out of the mind for the time being.

Week 5

Facing the Fears Head-on

Fear is our biggest enemy. Once you have broken the negative thought pattern, your mind will be able to think about things in a much better way. Yet, it may not be ready to shun all fears. If you are faced with situations that filled you with a sense of anxiety previously, they'll have the same impact again. The correct way to face fears is to experience and overcome them. However, this can't be done without preparation.

Facing Fears in a Safe Environment: The best way to move in this direction is to face your fears in a safe environment. If you feel that you have an intense fear of public speaking, begin by speaking only in front of a small group of your friends. When you see that you have a familiar group of faces that is even encouraging you, it'll be easier to give your first speech. Give a few speeches like than and then begin expanding the circle. Include a few people who are friends of friends and then strangers. When you move in a step-by-step manner in a safe environment conquering any fear becomes possible. The key is not to expose yourself to the fearful situation all at once but to do that gradually.

Week 6

Practice Relaxation

Completely relaxing the mind is the key to overcoming panic attacks, but this is just not a psychological process as there is biology involved too. As we have discussed, panic attacks can have some severe symptoms like shortness of breath, nausea, chest pain, etc. All these symptoms emerge because your body has a quick and severe response to a stressor. You must learn to keep the body relaxed to manage panic attacks successfully.

These relaxation techniques can help you in dealing with panic attacks is an amazing way. Not only will you feel more relaxed, but even the recovery from a panic attack would be very much easier.

Practice Relaxation Meditation: Relaxation meditation is the best when it comes to panic relief or relieving stress. It is easy and simple. You can practice it sitting or lying down as you feel comfortable. Just close your eyes and keep your awareness focused on a point. Keep breathing deeply and just push any thought that comes to mind. Your awareness should just focus on the point you are looking at with your eyes closed. Make everything else less important than this. This simple meditation will help you achieve a state of thoughtlessness.

Deep Breathing: This is one of the most important exercises in dealing with panic attacks or any other kind of anxiety. It is very simple and highly effective. You can follow it anywhere anytime. Whenever you feel a panic attack coming, you can start focusing on your breath and begin deep breathing. You'll see that a majority of times, you'll just not have a panic attack. Deep breathing is as simple as its name. Keep taking deep breaths in and then release your breath very slowly. You should also practice it at least once a day.

Progressive Muscle Relaxation: Stiffness of muscles is another cause of panic attacks. The pain and stiffness in the body keep getting ignored and emerges as a negative impulse. An easy way to get rid of that is to follow progressive muscle relaxation techniques. In this meditation technique, you scan your whole body through your awareness and release the pressure and anxiety built up in those areas. It gives you effective control of your body and also fills you up with a realization that there is no stress or anxiety inside you.

Meditation Using Guided Imagery: This is the best way to manage panic attacks. You can have a recorded guided meditation session using positive imagery liked by you. You'll be free to choose a location or situation of your choice. You can record it yourself or get a pre-recorded one. Whenever you fear a panic attack, you can switch on that guided meditation session, and the recollection of that happy place can help you avoid the negative thoughts that may lead to a panic attack.

Week 7

Practice Mindfulness

This week, you must practice mindfulness. Most people confuse meditation and mindfulness as being interchangeable terms, but they are not. Meditation is the art of looking inside. You don't run away from thoughts, you look inside the thoughts and try to understand them objectively. Mindfulness, on the other hand, is the practice of doing things mindfully. You stop running in an automated mode and start putting your consciousness behind every action you take.

For instance, when you eat, you pay attention to all the aspects of the food. You feel the taste, the aroma, the flavors, and the texture of the food. You pay attention to the process of eating. You chew the food properly and feel it while you chew. This process not only improves your understanding of every process, but it also helps in eliminating any kind of fear present in your mind regarding them.

Some Parts of Mindfulness Practice are:

Meditation: Be meditative in everything you do. Stop doing things in an automated mode. Take cognizance of every action you take.

Be Observant: Observe things more carefully and closely. Don't allow things to pass in front of you like that. Be observant of the things around you.

Stop Before Reacting: Before you react to anything, stop for a moment and think about that thing, the reaction it requires, and the kind of reaction you were going to give.

Learn to Shift Awareness: Learn the art of shifting your awareness on the object of your choice. For instance, if you are having fearful things about your flight, you should be able to fix your awareness at the swiftly moving second hand of your clock or any other such thing.

Week 8

Getting the Experience

This is the week to experience and practice all that you have learned in the past two months. The process may take a bit longer than two months in your case, but there is no need to worry as this is not to scale.

Just go out in the world and face your fear head-on.

However, you must observe the things you have been able to incorporate easily and the things that still need some work.

PART IV

Chapter 1: Self-Confidence In Various Situations

"Each time we face our fear, we gain strength, courage, and confidence in the doing."

-Theodore Roosevelt

While we have been speaking of self-worth and self-value, the focus of this chapter will be self-confidence, which is a different subject altogether.

Self-confidence is when you have faith in yourself and your abilities in a particular situation, and it does not relate to overall self-worth. If your self-confidence levels are low, it is because you are not comfortable in a particular setting, for whatever reason.

To help make self-confidence more clear, here are a few scenarios that showcase it in different circumstances.

- A doctor is self-confident when he performs any type of procedure within his specialty. He has so much training and experience that he truly believes in his skills and abilities to perform in various situations at work. When this same doctor goes for a hike, he does not have the same level of confidence in conquering a high peak, because he is out of shape.

- A mechanic can fix any car with his eyes closed. He has been a mechanic for so many years, that he is confident there is nothing that will come into his garage that he cannot handle. When this mechanic tries to work on the plumbing in his home, he is not very successful and has no confidence in his ability to perform the tasks.

- A great artist is confident in his ability to paint a portrait. If you ask him to solve a math problem, he has no confidence whatsoever.

These examples showcase how self-confidence can truly be based on the state of affairs, depending on what a person is facing at the moment. To handle a situation well, you must have self-confidence in your ability to do so. Self-confidence is gained through training, education, repetition, and life experience. It is impossible to be confident in every situation you ever come across, but the more you are willing to learn, the more confidence you will gain throughout life.

How a Lack of Self-Confidence Affects Us

As I mentioned before, self-confidence is circumstantial and will impact various areas of your life differently. Depending on how much experience, knowledge, or training, we have in different aspects of life, our confidence will ebb and flow. The key is to have self-confidence in the important areas of our lives, where it really matters. There are many examples in our everyday lives where self-confidence will play a major role.

Regarding the work setting, people who lack confidence in this arena cannot perform their necessary duties at an adequate level. This means poor job performance, being overlooked for raises and promotions, and even being let go from a position. If a person performs their job well, low self-confidence can still impact their desire to move up the latter. If they are confident in their particular position but do not feel confident at a higher level, like management, then they won't go after the promotion. They will simply stay put, even though they have the potential to do more.

Concerning starting a business, a certain level of confidence is needed to perform numerous tasks. There are many independent skills involved in running a business, and chances are, you will be doing most of them yourself when you first start. You need to have the proper training and education in these different areas, like finance, setting a budget, and marketing, etc., or you will not succeed in them. If you feel you can't do them yourself, then you may have to higher someone to do so. It may be worth it to avoid errors.

Self-confidence matters in our personal lives too. In order to find friends or develop relationships, we must have confidence in our abilities to form them. For example, it takes a lot of confidence for a man to walk up to a woman and say, "hi." To make friends, you must have the courage to talk to people. To learn new things and experience a new adventure, you must also have confidence in yourself to perform them. Once again, confidence comes from experience, and the more you put yourself out there, the more confident you will become.

Confidence is crucial in specific social settings. For example, during a work meeting, a lack of confidence can hold you back from speaking up, even if you have something very important to say. You won't get the necessary information out there that many people in the meeting could receive value from. This also relates to socializing with friends. You may have a friend who is harming themselves, but because you are uncertain how they will react, you ca nothing. You do not have the confidence that you will be able to respond appropriately.

A lack of confidence does not allow you to communicate assertively, which is important in order to get what you want. Instead of asking for things directly, you will beat around the bush and hope that the person will pick up on your clues. You will also use minimizing language, like "Sort of" or "kind of." This type of communication makes it seem like you lack conviction, and no one will take you seriously. You will just appear weak. Being assertive is essential, whether you are asking for something at working or setting boundaries with your friends.

If you suffer from low self-confidence, then every aspect of your life will suffer. We will get into different ways of increasing your confidence in the next chapter. For now, we will discuss how self-confidence works in different settings, especially in those that create anxiety for everybody.

Chapter 2: Social Anxiety

For this chapter, I will provide more detail for a specific type of confidence issue, and that is social anxiety.

Social Anxiety and Lack of Confidence In Specific Situations

Social anxiety is an actual disorder where a person has a phobia in which a person feels like they are being watched and judged by everybody. There may be select situations where this is actually happening, but in most circumstances, it is an unfound fear. This is an extreme situation where a person has a lack of confidence in everything they do, and therefore, feel like they are the center of attention.

Going for a job interview, taking a test, going on a date, or speaking in public are normal things that create anxiety in almost everybody. It is amplified greatly in someone who has a social anxiety disorder. Furthermore, these individuals actually become nervous during normal, everyday activities like shopping for food, parking their car, or using a public restroom. Their anxiety is so intense that they feel judged in every moment of their lives. This fear can become so strong that it interferes with people going to work, attending school, talking to their friends, or doing any other menial task during the day.

It is estimated that about seven percent of the American population suffers from social anxiety. While this number is not massive, it shows that the problem is not uncommon.

Researchers believe there is a genetic component where areas of the brain that deal with fear and anxiety are involved. However, there is no explanation as to why some family members are affected while others are not. For example, out of two siblings, one may be shy and quiet, while the other one is loud and bombastic.

Another cause of social anxiety may be underdeveloped social skills. Some individuals will feel discouraged after talking to people, even if the conversation did not go poorly, which will cause them to avoid interactions in the future. The lack of interaction will just lead to further underdeveloped social skills, and the social anxiety trend will continue.

Many people with this disorder do not have anxiety in specific social settings, but instead in areas where performance is involved. This is often referred to as performance anxiety and is related to performing in front of a crowd in any type of capacity, whether it is a speech, dance recital, or sporting event. Speaking in public is one of the worst fears that people have, and in some surveys, it is number one. Jerry Seinfeld used to make the joke that during a funeral, most people would rather be inside the casket than the ones giving the eulogy.

Even if a person is confident in the subject matter, having to discuss it in a large crowd, with hundreds, or even thousands, of eyes, looking at them, will create a high level of anxiety. This situation would be unsettling for many people. There are many reasons why someone would have a fear of speaking in public, and it goes beyond just being nervous.

Fear and anxiety will create a physiological response within us. During this process, our autonomic nervous system, which works as a protective mechanism by keeping us alert, will make us hyper-arousable. Generally, this is done to put the body in a state of battle. As a result, we will have an emotional experience to fear, which will interfere with our ability to perform well in front of an audience.

Another factor to consider is the person's beliefs about the speaking engagement. Many people will feel that if they screw up something in front of a crowd, it will hurt their credibility, and therefore, their careers. They also feel that their performance will never be forgotten, and their whole public image will be destroyed in an instant. The fact that everyone has a camera on their phones lends some more credibility to this fear. These feelings cause people to overthink and become extremely anxious beyond their control.

Anxiety during a public speech is greater in those who don't do it often. The more a person speaks in front of a crowd, the less nervous they become over time. Unfortunately, most people do not speak in front of audiences constantly, unless they do it for a living. If someone only speaks a few times a year or less, then they will usually have anxiety every time. Also, a person's status in relation to the audience members can play a role in their confidence levels. For example, if a person is speaking in front of high-level executives about a topic they already know, then this can create an immense amount of fear. They worry about having their speech dissected. What a person must realize here is that it is not so much the content of the speech, but how it is presented.

The most obvious reason for the fear of public speaking is the actual skill involved. Speaking in front of an audience involves getting the people engaged. This is done by proper timing, eye contact, stage presences, charisma, and a little bit of humor. The bottom line is, you must be able to connect with the audience somehow, or they will not care whatsoever what you have to say, no matter who you are. Your status may capture their attention for a while, but if you can't keep their attention, your speech will be forgotten before it even starts. Many people know this and are worried that they won't be able to hold their audience's attention.

The more anxious you are, the less likely you are to perform well. It is to your advantage to be as relaxed as possible and overcome your social anxiety, which is much easier said than done.

Aside from public speaking, another social situation that can cause anxiety is being in a large crowd. Many people with social anxiety are okay when they are just around their friends. However, once the circle starts increasing, their anxiety grows tremendously. This type of fear is known as enochlophobia, and it is related to the perceived dangers posed by large gatherings of people you may see in everyday life. The fear includes getting lost, stuck, or harmed in some manner by the crowd.

Most of you are probably thinking of concerts or other places where organized gatherings occur. The simple solution here would be to avoid these types of events. However, this fear also encompasses busy metropolitan areas, public transits like the bus or subway, or even workspaces with a lot of employees. Any type of space where a large number of people are, a person with this type of phobia will become fearful and anxious.

In the next chapter, we will describe various ways to build up your self-confidence, so you can be prepared to handle any situation, even if you are not familiar with it.

Chapter 3: Learning to Become Comfortable

When you lack self-confidence, it means you are unsure of yourself in a particular setting. You have a certain level of discomfort, which precludes you from going all-in when performing a certain task. Unfortunately, if your confidence levels are not high enough, then you will not perform at your highest level. This does not mean you aren't nervous or slightly anxious. It literally means that you do not believe in yourself in a specific situation.

A person will never feel fully confident in every aspect of life. There will be plenty of times when we are faced with something new, and it will completely throw us off our game. The goal of this chapter will be to build self-esteem in some of the most important areas of our lives and also develop the critical thinking skills we need to overcome almost any situation, no matter how unfamiliar it may be.

Building Your Self-Confidence

Nobody is born with an unlimited amount of self-confidence. Also, people are not born with zero confidence. It is something that either gets built-up or deteriorated over time. Unfortunately, many people have had their confidence shattered so many times that they never have confidence in themselves in any situation, no matter how familiar they are with it. The practices in this section will focus on building self-confidence in the general sense, so you are ready to attack life, no matter what gets thrown your way.

Groom Yourself Regularly

This may sound obvious, but many people do not realize how good they will feel when they take the time to shower, do their hair, clean their nails, and dress nicely. The old saying, "When you look good, you feel good," Holds a lot of truth. Even if you have nothing important planned for the day, take the time to groom yourself. You will automatically feel more confident in any situation you come across. You don't have to go to the salon every day or wear thousand-dollar suits. The goal is to look good when you observe yourself in the mirror. This could mean wearing your favorite shirt and jeans combination.

Photoshop Your Self-Image

We take a lot of stock in our self-image. No matter how much we try to say that looks don't matter, we like to look at ourselves in the mirror and see a positive self-image. You can alter your self-image by mentally photoshopping yourself in a way that is positive to you. You can then work on obtaining this image in real-life. For example, if you see yourself 20 pounds lighter, then keep this image in your mind and work towards it.

Destroy Negative Thoughts

No matter how unfamiliar you are with a situation, you are more likely to handle it well if you get rid of your negative thoughts. These simply take up space in your mind and have no value in your productivity. Be aware of our self-talk and how you think about yourself. This may sound ridiculous, but when you find a negative thought entering your mind, picture it as an object or creature that you want to destroy. For example, when you begin having negative thoughts, picture them as bugs. Now, squash those bugs mentally, and you will effectively destroy your negative thoughts. This is a great mental trick to play on yourself. After getting rid of the negative thought, replace it with a positive one.

Get to Know Yourself

When going into battle, it is best to know your enemy very well, no matter who they are. When you are dealing with low self-confidence, your enemy becomes yourself. This is why it is important to get to know yourself as well as you can. Listen intently to your thoughts, write about yourself in a journal, determine what thoughts about yourself dominate your mind, and analyze why you have negative thoughts.

Next, write down all of the positive aspects that you have, no matter how minuscule they may seem. Start thinking about the limitations you have and determine if they are real and verified, or just something you came up with in your head. Dig as deep you can get into your psyche, and you will find out more about yourself than you had ever known. The more you know about yourself, the greater self-confidence you will have.

Be Kind and Generous

Be kind and generous to others, whether it is time, money, or other resources, will be great for improving your self-image. When you are genuinely able to help someone when they need you, then it makes you feel good about who you are. It gives you a sense of purpose.

Be Prepared

Be as prepared for life as you can. Think about this for a moment: if you are taking an exam, and have not studied, then you won't be prepared, and your confidence level will be very low. On the other hand, if you did study intensely, then you will be much more prepared and have a greater amount of confidence. Imagine life as one big exam. The more prepared you are every day, the more confident you will feel in any situation. The following are some general ways you can be more prepared.

- Have plenty of food in the refrigerator and cabinets.
- Have a substantial emergency fund.
- Have the basics as far as emergency supplies at all times.
- If you have something specific planned for that day, like a presentation or meeting, be as prepared as possible for it.
- Always be on alert for dangerous situations.

Know Your Principles and Live By Them

What are the main principles upon which your life is built? If you are not sure, then it's time to sit down and really think about it. Otherwise, your life will be completely directionless. When you know your principles and live by them, then you are truly living your passion, and this is great for your self-confidence. People who are simply coasting through life with no real values will have no goals in life either. They are simply existing and not fully living. When you refuse to live your life based on your values, then you lack confidence in yourself.

Speak Slowly

Speaking slowly will make a huge difference in how people perceive you. It shows a sense of knowledge and confidence in what is being said. Someone who speaks with a rapid-fire approach generally does so because they are not confident in what they are saying. They just want to get the word out there and hope nobody calls them out. Even if you don't feel totally confident on a subject, try speaking slowly anyway, and see how much your self-confidence actually builds. This can be a great mind trick. When you speak slow, you have more time to formulate good thoughts. Of course, I am not telling you to take it to the extreme here, just don't spit words out like a machine gun.

Stand Up Straight

This is another simple trick to help you feel better about yourself. When you slouch, not only does it showcase a lack of confidence, you actually have less self-confidence. This goes along the lines of looking good and feeling good. And trust me, when you stand up straighter, you will look much better.

Increase Your Competence Levels

Simply put, if you are more competent in something, you feel more confident. You gain competence through practice and training. In any situation in life, get as much training as you can to feel as fully self-confident as you can. Let's use the example of a house fire. I hope that your house never burns down, but if it does, I want you to feel confident that you and your family can escape safely. Map out an escape plan and practice it as often as you can. Many companies do quarterly evacuation drills. Employ this same practice in your house. If an emergency like this ever occurs, you will have more competence, and therefore, confidence in being able to handle it. Think of as many possible circumstances as you can in life, and determine ways to practice and train in them.

Set Small Goals and Achieve Them

When you are able to achieve a goal in life, it is a huge boost to your confidence. Set small goals regularly and then work hard to accomplish them. Remember, they should be small and reasonable. You can even cut down larger goals into smaller achievable steps. For example, if your goal is to buy a car, you can create a goal to save a certain amount of money by the end of the month, and then every month after that.

Change Small Habits About Yourself

Trying to change a large habit all at once can be very difficult, and the chances of failure are high. This will be a huge shot to your confidence. Instead, focus on smaller habits that will lead to big change. For example, if your goal is to wake up early and workout before starting your day, then don't try to wake up two hours earlier on the first day. Start by waking up 10-20 minutes early until it becomes a habit, and then increase the time from there as you feel comfortable.

Focus Your Attention on Solutions

So often, we are completely focused on the problems and pay no attention to the solutions. For example, you may always complain about being tired, but do nothing to change it, because the solutions never enter your mind. Make it a habit to focus on solutions whenever a problem enters your mind. You will get more accomplished and gain a lot of self-confidence. For example, if you are tired every day, then what is making you that way. Are you not sleeping enough? If not, then why is that? Are you eating too much sugar before going to bed? Do you have a poor diet during the day? Are you drinking enough water? See how man questions you can get answered if you just shift your focus from the problems to the solutions. Try it out with any small problems that you may have and notice the results.

Become Active

You may have noticed that when you start taking action, work starts getting done. So often, people sit around and worry about how they will get something done, rather than doing the work to get it done. Excessive worry leads to a lack of confidence. The more you worry, the lower your self-confidence will become. If you take action, you will obtain results. Results lead to increased confidence. Next time you find yourself worrying about something, start developing a plan and execute it. Hours of taking actions will give you better results than hours of sitting around and worrying.

Gain More Knowledge

Empowering yourself with knowledge is one of the greatest ways to build self-confidence. You will never know everything, but the more you know, the better you will feel about yourself. This goes along the same vein as building competence. You become more knowledgeable on a subject by studying and practicing it. This does not have to be something you will use. It can just be for your own self-fulfillment. According to psychology, one of the biggest reasons for low self-confidence is either misinformation or a lack of information. As you become more empowered with knowledge, you will gain more information too.

Just like with the steps to gain self-esteem, these previous steps must be employed regularly. Our self-confidence will be challenged all the time, so it is in our best interest to build it up regularly through practice and discipline. Think of your confidence as a muscle that you must work out every single day. Do this, and you will be amazed at how much self-confidence you have throughout your life.

Overcoming Procrastination

People love to procrastinate. And why wouldn't they? Why do something now if you can do it tomorrow? I'll tell you why. What keeps you from making the same excuse tomorrow? Also, how do you know what tomorrow will bring? Perhaps something will happen that prevents you from doing the task then, too. A better question to ask yourself is: Why wait until tomorrow if you can get it done now.

Procrastination is a huge problem in our society, and it leads to a lot of anxiety. This anxiety, in turn, leads to a lack of self-confidence. Procrastination is basically a form of being unprepared. Let's say you have a project due on Friday, and it is now Monday. If you begin working on it now, and do a little bit each day, you will have more confidence in completing the project and doing it well, than you would if you started on Thursday. Imagine how much more thorough you can be by starting projects a little bit earlier. The following are a few easy action steps you can take to help overcome procrastination.

- Do not take on more than you can handle. Keep the number of decisions you have to make to a minimum. The more you have to decide on, the more likely you are to procrastinate.

- Begin focusing on the benefits of completing something, rather than the task. For example, if you are working on a project for work, imagine how good it will feel when it's done. Also, think about the rewards that might come if you perform the task well, like a promotion or raise. This focus on the benefits will give you more motivation to get started.

- Prepare yourself for a task by becoming educated on it. Be aware of your limitations before even picking up a new project and do what you can to obtain the necessary knowledge before moving forward. Once again, knowledge will lead to confidence, and confidence makes you active in a pursuit.

- Turn distractions into rewards. If you cannot get your work done because you are always binge-watching shows, then force yourself to turn them into rewards after a hard day's work. For example, set a timer for three hours and use that time to focus on your projects. After the three hours, pat yourself on the back and watch an episode of the show you like. Remember that you have to stay disciplined.

- Set up a daily schedule system for yourself. For example, the first two hours in the morning are designated for the most important tasks, then a break, followed by two hours of the less important tasks, then another break, and finally, dedicating the last part of the day towards the least important tasks. Once you set up a schedule, stick to it to the best of your ability.
- Avoid getting stuck on a project. Give yourself a certain amount of time on a specific task, and if you cannot make progress, move onto something else and revisit it later. There is no sense in wasting time being nonproductive on something.

Follow these steps religiously and watch procrastination be an afterthought in your life.

Build Confidence At Work

Our jobs are a major part of our lives, and it is important to have self-confidence in this environment. We went over building self-confidence in the general sense earlier in this chapter, and now we will focus on more specific areas in our lives. Many of the action steps and techniques are still the same, while some will be more geared towards work.

- Cut out the negative self-talk. Do not beat yourself up at work. It will do nothing for you. Speaking kindly and encouragingly to yourself and you will learn from whatever mistakes you made more easily.

- Boost your knowledge any way you can, and it is a surefire way to achieve confidence. Stay up on the latest research, services, and products within your company and industry as a whole. Imagine being able to bring an idea to your workplace simply because you read up on it. This will make you feel very good about yourself. Always try to stay ahead of the curve.

- Use opportunities to teach others who know less about a subject than you do. Being able to teach others effectively will boot your own knowledge and confidence.

- Practice what you know incessantly, and always look for ways to improve. Identify and correct mistakes along the way.

- Do not speak poorly about others. This already shows a lack of confidence in yourself. When you compliment and speak highly of other people, you acknowledge their strengths and make them feel good about themselves. In turn, you feel good about yourself, too. This also helps to build a nontoxic work environment.

- Pick up new skills to enhance proficiency at your job.

- Ask questions when you do not know something. You may think that you will feel stupid if you ask a question. However, asking and then doing it right, is a bigger boost to confidence than not asking and screwing things up.

- Eliminate negative language, even if it's not geared at anybody. Negative language can affect our psyche on the deepest levels, effectively lowering our confidence levels without us even realizing it.

- Focus on all of the success you have had at work, rather than the failures.

Chapter 4: Getting Rid of Social Anxiety

Social anxiety encompasses many areas of our lives, such as personal relationships, engaging in activities, hanging out in large groups, or giving public speeches. In order to engage in any of these areas, we must overcome our social anxiety, which is essentially having a lack of confidence in social settings. Depending on the individual, social anxiety will either impact them no matter what setting they're, while for others, it will be more selective. For example, a person may be very talkative and confident among his friends but will be terrified when speaking or performing on stage.

This can be the other way around, too. Legendary late-night host, Johnny Carson, was magnanimous on stage but known to be quiet, reserved, and even shy in small groups. We will go over some basic techniques to improve your social anxiety. These will be effective in just about any setting you are in. These techniques are involved with cognitive behavioral therapy, which is a psychologically-based approach to dealing with anxiety, that is drugfree.

- Think about what you're avoiding. As always, the first step in solving a problem is by identifying what it is. What specific social settings are you avoiding. For instance, some people have stated things like using a public restroom, ordering food at a restaurant, becoming scared in a large group, or speaking up at a meeting. Determine what settings cause your social anxiety. Write these down somewhere so you can keep track.

- Now, take your list that you made and develop some type of rating system. This is used to determine the level of anxiety you might experience in each situation to determine what makes it worse. If you feel the most anxious while giving a public speech, then you can rate that as a 10, and then move down from there. So if being around friends gives you none or very little anxiety, that can be a 0 or 1 rating. These ratings are based mainly on predictions. Basically, we are predicting how we would react in certain social settings.

- The next step is to test your predictions. Go out and put yourself in specific situations that may or may not give you the level of anxiety you predicted. For instance, you may have thought you would be at a level of 9 when meeting someone new at a party, but once you did, it was actually around a 4 rating. You may surprise yourself at how well you can actually cope with your anxiety.

- Identify safety behaviors that you use and work to eliminate them. These are superstitious behaviors that people engage in to make them feel safer. I am not talking about carrying a rabbit's foot. Safety behaviors are things like pre-medicating before a social event, avoiding eye contact, rehearsing what you're going to say, or walking with stiff shoulders. The main problem with these types of behaviors is that you will believe they are the only way to get through an anxiety-casing situation. The more you give up these behaviors, the better your experience will be. Imagine how much better a conversation will be when it's natural, rather than scripted.

- Challenge your anxious thoughts. Instead of thinking about how bad things will go, start thinking about how they will go well. If you are worried about looking foolish, ask yourself why that is, and when have you actually looked foolish in the past? Is it real or made up in your head.

- Practice doing what makes you anxious. The classic example here is giving a speech in front of a mirror or recording yourself while you speak alone in your living room. Remind yourself that people don't usually know what your internal feelings are unless you make it obvious to them. This means that no one may have noticed your anxiety in the past. Eventually, test out what you've practiced in the real world. In the case of a speech, after practicing alone for a while, you can perform it in front of some friends.

- Practice self-reward, rather than post-mortem. Post-mortem means that a person analyzes and criticizes every little thing that they've done during a social encounter. If they were standing awkwardly, they become focused on that. Instead, reward yourself for facing the anxiety-causing situation.

Remember to always rinse and repeat with all of these techniques. They must be done regularly until you develop a pattern. You will never be fully confident in every situation. The world will throw things at you that will make you take a few steps back and throw you off your game. That is okay. The key to these exercises is to build up a certain level of self-confidence so that you will be ready to engage and deal with whatever life throws at you. You will develop true strength and knowledge to overcome, no matter how unfamiliar a situation is.